Thinking into Success

Your Awareness defines your Success...

By
Suryaprabha Easwar

Copyright © 2023 by – Suryaprabha Easwar - All Rights Reserved.

Dedication

The book is devoted to H.E. Sheikh. Zayed bin Sultan Al Nahyan, Founding Father of the United Arab Emirates. The country is a live example of how visioneering and creative thinking can transform even a desert into an architectural masterpiece and a world-wide attraction, be it for Tourism, Global Investments, Science and Technology, Art, and culture, enabling rapid economic and impactful development of the Middle East.

Acknowledgment

I would like to thank my mentors, Bob Procter and Mary Morrissey, for their inspiration, study materials, and guidance throughout my research journey. I also take this opportunity to thank my publisher Amazon Publishers Pro, who so diligently and efficiently helped me self-publish this book seamlessly.

Preface

This book provides awareness and simple and practical guidance on how to find life's purpose and how one can achieve success in any endeavor through Creative Living, i.e., living *Inside Out* in the face of extreme external circumstances. This is a sequel to my previous book, *Thinking into Desires*. By continuous self-development and application of divergent thinking, as explained in the chapters of this book, one can attain both spiritual enlightenment as well material success at the same time. From my own experience, I can say this is very much possible!

The life force that created us requires us to continue to create, which is the fundamental Law of the Universe. Everyone must be aware of their Right to Riches. It is an absolute myth that only chosen few can have all the abundance, power, and wealth. Humans were created by the Omnipotent power of God as a perfect package with all the tools required for limitless growth potential, which explains the rise of the cave-man to a Space explorer. We are blessed with six beautiful mental faculties, i.e., – *Reasoning, Imagination, Memory, Will, Intuition, and Perception*, which need to be trained and used to the fullest. We don't have to do certain things, but we do things in a certain way to achieve the desired results and attain bliss in whatever we do. These certain ways are articulated within the Eleven Laws of Life, such as the Law of Vibration, Law of Obedience, Law of Compensation, and Law of Receiving, which the book introduces to the readers in simple language for easy application. There is nothing happening by force;

you let things come to you by changing your self-image. By using and practicing these laws and tools, one can start manifesting abundance and opportunities very quickly in all aspects of their life.

I have also attempted to clear certain social and cultural myths and paradigms using personal experiences and illustration based on my interpretation of works of great Thinkers and Writers such as Bob Procter, Neville Goddard, Napoleon Hill, Raymond Holliwell, and Viktor Frankl, as their teachings and studies have greatly inspired and contributed immensely to raising my own awareness. Repeated and continuous study of this book and its concepts within will gradually change the mindset resulting in raised self-image and transformed external results in life.

I heartily thank Amazon Publishers Pro for standing by me and patiently guiding me through the process of publishing this book.

All beings are just one,

created from one common power!

Only man, but has the gift

to change the flow of events

by thinking wise or otherwise,

to make him a fortune

or to make him poor!

- **Suryaprabha Easwar**

Table of Contents

Dedication ii

Acknowledgment iii

Preface vi

Chapter 1 What is Success? 1

Chapter 2 Awareness 7

Chapter 3 Self-Image and Attitude 14

Chapter 4 Vision, Goal, and Purpose 22

Chapter 5 Your Frequency 31

Chapter 6 Laws of the Universe 40

Chapter 7 Belief & Faith 54

Chapter 8 Fear and Courage 60

Chapter 9 Living Inside out - Imagination 66

Chapter 10 Focus and Will 75

Chapter 11 Generative Gratitude 82

Chapter 12 Calmness of Mind 89

About the Author 95

Chapter 1
What is Success?

Success is indeed a very elusive word. It may be defined in countless ways depending on each person's perception and level of Awareness. If you ask fifty passersby, each will have their own unique opinion on this. The way one defines success often will contradict what someone else says based on their own beliefs, value systems, culture, knowledge, etc. People tend to see *success* both objectively and subjectively. For every one of us, during our lifetime, the meaning attached to Successful Life significantly changes as years roll by between our teenage to mid-forties or fifties.

From an objective standpoint, people tend to link salary, job title, business income, prestigious company, awards, career progress, and accolades to success. While personally, they would link sports or vocational activities, fitness, and family activities such as holidays and retirement savings as success criteria. These perceptions about success and unique definitions are embedded in your mind from young childhood based on ideas, culture, and social and economic circumstances during growth and adulthood. In other words, the definition is built on inputs received from external feed, which later becomes an inseparable part of the person's character and lifestyle. From a subjective viewpoint, which usually happens to be part two of the Awareness level, when people get a little older and more experienced, they tend to start thinking about the ability to relax and recharge, fulfilling relationships, children's success, and so forth. As a natural process, due to changes in Awareness levels, people start perceiving things differently.

But the underlying beliefs are quite similar for 95% of the population. Most people are playing the world's most popular game – *follow the followers* - they consider success to be something that normally other people do. However, this really will not take one too far, as there is nothing creative in this kind of living. The life force that created us requires us to continue to create, which is the fundamental Law of the Universe. The universe itself is an infinitely expanding tapestry, as science has shown us. By following the footsteps of general folks, we tend to convince ourselves that we are living a wholesome life, only to be subsequently left with dissatisfaction, emptiness, and depression, thinking about how we wish we can or could have lived differently. There is an unexplained hurtful void created by such mediocre living.

Hence Awareness of the laws of life is crucial along with the roadmap to a successful life which is what this book is all about. The Laws are detailed in a later chapter; however, first, it is imperative to clearly understand the meaning of success. Several personal development experts have researched this topic for years over the last century, and after seventeen years of extensive research, great American Personal Development and Motivational Author and Speaker Earl Nightingale defined success in his book *The Strangest Secret* in 1957 as follows:

> *"Success is Progressive Realization of a Worthy Ideal."*

Simple but a very profound definition. This is the best-known definition and most relevant for all ages. The definition is so simple, undisputable, and applies to everyone, irrespective of whether a child, student, salesman, politician, housewife, or artist. Let us break down and analyze the various parts of this definition:

Progressive, Realization, Worthy, and Ideal.

Progressive means continuously moving forward. The spirit or life force inside each one of us always wants fuller expression and expansion in whatever we do - the chosen field, vocation, business, service, or simply any endeavor. There are infinite levels of learning which means there is no end to it. As the Universe itself is always in a state of expansion, its nature reflects in its creations, too; that is our true inner power; our own creative power also wants to expand and grow infinitely. So, life **must** be progressive and forward-moving. What can be a better example of success than this - A zygote, by the process of cell division, develops into a full-term baby, landing on the earth one fine day, learning to roll over, then sit, stand, and slowly learn to walk and run. An artist achieves mastery of painting progressively over a span of a few years. A businessperson starting a small establishment and then expanding his business worldwide. A student progresses in school through various levels and then finishes college. This is what progress is – and it is the first component of success.

Realization means manifestation. In other words, achievement. Realization can be in many forms; this could be milestones met, a larger customer or fan base, more money, fame, rewards and awards, windfall contracts, a house, cars, in fact, anything that produces a tangible or intangible result of your action or service to yourself and the people who receive the benefit. It is a progressive realization, so it happens in a row, a series of manifestations one after another, in other words – accomplishing continuously. The child's state is continuously changing from one stage to another, the artist's level of mastery is changing continuously over many years, and the businessman's size and client base, turnover, and profits are constantly changing. This realization or change in state is the second critical component of success. Some like to call it a *measure* of success.

<u>Worthy</u>– What is worthy? Who's worth? Worthy is something that gives benefit and value to one or many and is produced legitimately. The larger the number of people that benefit from the service or product, the more worthy it is!! Or in other words, the greater the impact of the service or action on positively influencing the world, the more worthy it is. Why do World-Renowned Top-Ranking Singers earn millions of dollars just for a four-minute hit song while a particularly good artist in a small remote town earns a meager income that barely meets his daily needs? It's because of the nature of service: how much happiness, emotion, positivity, and value a service or product generates define its true worthiness. Mother Teresa's life was highly successful in achieving her life's purpose – to help the poor and needy across the world. It is self-explanatory in terms of its worthiness; she was remarkably successful and received Nobel Prize for her humanitarian contributions. The birth of a baby is also a worthy act of creating a life on earth as it aligns with the laws of the Universe, which is the constant and creative expansion and growth. Trees grow, animals grow, and landforms change their states due to tectonic movement. These are the Laws of the Universe. Similarly, the businessperson creates value for clients and, in return, earns his rewards in the form of profits. He creates employment opportunities, adds to economic transactions, and thus helps in the country's progress.

<u>Ideal</u> – The most important part of the definition, indeed! An ideal is an *idea that you love*. An ideal is a spark of thought with which we fall in love. It is a passionate goal. It is charged with much more spiritual value than a common goal. Passion leads to progressive learning, which leads to experience, then to excellence and mastery, which

automatically attracts success, rewards including financial gains, and well-being. In the example of Mother Teresa stated earlier, from her point of view, the happiness and contentment she got by serving the needy was the biggest reward. On the other hand, to those around her, her popularity, acknowledgements, and awards may appear to be her success.

For me, writing this book and getting it published is indeed a great success – as it has all the four components stated above. The fact that I am able to study, write, and share my self-help books with the world gives me immense joy and satisfaction. That is my greatest reward for writing these books – my worthy ideal.

In all instances, we notice a flow, movement, and continuity. So, we can also say - Success is a running and unlimited process - the only constant being *progressive realization*; in other words, a journey with experience and knowledge collected along the way. It is with this understanding that great American professional tennis player Arthur Robert Ashe Jr., winner of three Grand Slam singles titles, rightly said:

> *"Success is a journey, not a Destination."*

It is very important, however, to point out one thing before moving on. *Realization* – the second word in the definition, It has two parts to it – one is the ability to conclude the desired action or service or create the desired product (for example, a baby learns to walk, I write a book), and the second the resultant benefit or changes that will take place in people's lives due to that (bliss, well-being, health, wealth and so on). When you think of buying a car, your family will benefit from it; it's worthy for your family – but when you think of setting up a car factory, you facilitate hundreds of others to earn and buy their own cars. So, a Worthy Ideal is really a Big Idea that you love and benefits a larger number of people.

Going by this simplified and crisp definition of success, one can not only easily find his or her worthy ideal but also be sure of going in the right direction. This simple definition helps redefine success in the reader's life, be it an employee, businessman, housewife, schoolteacher, singer, and so on. The worthy ideal may vary from person to person and cannot be tied down to either of two extremes – 1. Only Focusing on making more money, 2. Giving up all personal desires, including money, for other people's benefit. Both these would be against the laws of the Universe. The joy lies in between, in the balance. We must endeavor to find this Balance. One, therefore, needs to be quite careful in choosing the worthy ideal. That is where our Thinking faculty comes in. How can you think yourself into success? Let's explore this in the upcoming chapters.

Chapter 2 Awareness

The subject of Awareness and Consciousness has been analyzed and researched to a great extent by philosophers, scientists, psychologists, and many others. Despite this wealth of ideas and understanding, *consciousness* remains an unsolved mystery for mankind. The purpose of this chapter is not to get into any debate about the true meaning of consciousness but to emphasize the importance of raising the consciousness level, i.e., Awareness, and how this act of successfully changing the awareness level can result in changing various aspects of our life. So, we stick to the simplest definition of consciousness, i.e., the <u>*sense of knowing*</u> within the boundaries of the Mind.

To understand how self-development can be achieved by raising the level of consciousness, we must review the correlation between Mind and Thought first. Mind is not matter; it does not have a structure; it is not your brain. It is a spiritual and non-physical potent powerhouse. It exists all around us and inside of us at the same time. It is part of the universal intelligence that originally wrote the pattern plan for life on earth. It is there in our DNA, in a hen's egg, in an acorn, in you and me too! Nobody has ever seen the mind, and hence it cannot be drawn or reproduced by anyone. However, a human mind can *think*. And thought is an energy just like light and electric energy. Thought waves are potent, immensely powerful, and can transcend all time and space at once. It has been proved scientifically that thought waves can travel faster than light or sound waves even. The most comfortable and sensible assumption, therefore, would be that the mind is simply a movement or an activity where Thoughts originate. It's a powerhouse of Thought energy.

It is important to note that while the *mind is an activity*, the *body is the manifestation of the activity*. As science tells us, the human body is nothing but a mass of molecules vibrating at a very high frequency. The level of frequency indicates the level of awareness one has about the world in which he or she lives. There are infinite levels of Awareness, the lowest being zero frequency when you do not move at all, no consciousness, no awareness; there is no life in that zone. The happy, abundant, and successful life sits on the higher rung of the awareness ladder. So the more aware one is, the more successful he/she becomes. The highest level is the Divinity of the Omnipotent power that created us all. We shall talk about Frequency in greater detail later in Chapter 5 of this book. Just want to emphasize here the importance of raising awareness levels. This book will change your belief:

> **"Ignorance is _not_ a Bliss"**

It has been reiterated by great thinkers and authors that: *Both the creator and the creation are the same mind.* Anything that is created is a product of the mind that originated in a thought sometime, somewhere. Look at everything around you, the pen that you are holding, your laptop or mobile, the lamps in your room, doorknobs and bells, the buildings around you, your car, the airplanes; all these once originated in thought. They then became a reality after years of effort and focused study on the same subject. Now let us see how the thought energy flows to manifest results in life.

The following illustration depicts an important piece of knowledge that is the foundation for all the other takeaways from this book for personal development and success.

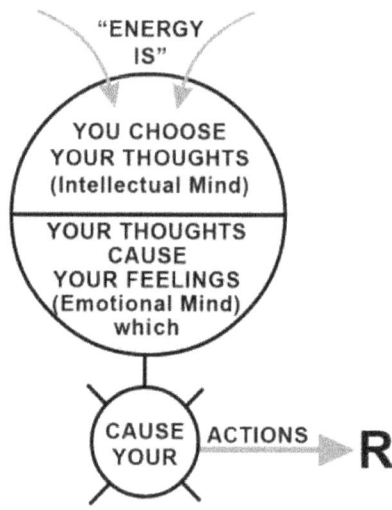

Source: Procter Gallagher Institute of Personal Development

The R in the above picture represents Results in life. Thomas Alva Edison believed that a light bulb could be designed from electrical energy, then studied it for a prolonged period failing nine hundred and ninety-nine times before it finally worked. The electric energy and the laws that govern the flow of that energy were always there; it is only in the last hundred years or so that we became aware of how to harness it, use the knowledge of conductivity and insulation to make a light bulb, i.e., became aware of it. All the abundance and riches already exist in our environment, but you must be aware of your Right to Riches. As stated by Wallace D Wattle: *A person's right to life means his right to have the free and unrestricted use of all the things which may be necessary to his fullest mental, spiritual, and physical unfolding – in other words, his right to be rich.*

One must clearly understand that regardless of your present situation in life, wanting to win, to be successful, and to dream of living in luxury is not foolish or ridiculous. It is as natural as the night following the day. Man is matter and passes through different states by virtue of his beliefs and thoughts throughout his lifetime. Each state constitutes a level of Awareness. The higher the level of Awareness, the better the life. As Bob Procter, the great Canadian Thinker and Self Development guru rightly points out – *One does not earn the income he earns currently because he wants to earn this but because he does not know how to earn ten times the same income.*

Another key point to be aware of is the gift of mental faculties. Let me bust this myth for you now – Many people say that - *We come to this world empty-handed and shall depart empty-handed – so why make all the effort working hard and amassing wealth, making great accomplishments?* This thinking is sinful and against the Laws of the Universe. We do not come empty-handed, nor shall we go empty-handed from this earth. We were created as a perfect package with all the tools required for limitless growth potential. We as human beings are the highest form of God's creation and gifted with six beautiful mental faculties that are – *Reasoning, Imagination, Memory, Will, Intuition, and Perception.* Readers are urged to make special note of these faculties. How much progress you make in life depends on how much you train and exercise these faculties. All great men, scientists, and achievers in different fields have used one or more of these proficiently, enabling them to make such great contributions. These faculties, my dear readers, are the secret gateways to success and inbuilt in us. In other words, we are already born rich! However, these need to be exercised and trained, as these are like any other muscles in our body.

Secondly, when we die, while we cannot carry our material wealth with us, what remains permanently tied to us will be the recognition and the contribution that we have made to mankind. No one can take that away from us. You see, man's intelligence is constantly expanding, and we are advancing in every field. Be it Science, Technology, Art, Space studies, or any field. The knowledge that we leave behind will be used by the next generation to develop further. We cannot forget Marconi, Edison, and Henry Ford for their valuable contributions. The next generation of great thinkers shall build upon the knowledge and idea to make further inventions for the betterment of civilization. These great men will never die – their image will keep flickering on the screens of our minds for their great work. In fact, they become immortals. So, one can die leaving behind a rich legacy of knowledge and awareness which is inexhaustible; they didn't die empty-handed!!

We must be aware of our inner strengths and respect and train them adequately to create value for both us and the world around us. It is each and everyone's responsibility to use the gift of mental faculties as much as you can and share your knowledge as much as possible, not just keep it to oneself and die with all the resources locked in their bones!

> *"Your Awareness is your legacy."*

Awareness has no limit; hence mastery could be a near-impossible feat, but what is more important is the endeavor to expand and grow. The intention must always be to progress by developing Awareness, which is the first and foremost piece in solving the Success puzzle in one's life! I have an unsatiating quest to continuously learn about the laws of life, and this is my life's purpose too. When you fully surrender to your worthy ideal (as defined in chapter 1), you open the gateway of free flow of energy from the Spiritual (non-physical) to the physical world, and the manifestation of your intent happens as *Results* in your life.

To follow one's worthy ideal, it is important to choose one first. How do you choose your Ideal?

Ideas are like slippery fish that will slip out of your mind if you do not pin them down with a pencil – Earl Nightingale.

Ideas float in the ethereal cloud and are available to us 24X7 through thoughts. While Money is Man's currency, Ideas are god's currency – it is unlimited, infinite, and have all the creative power of God packed in them – waiting to be manifested in physical form.

It is also very important for us to be able to distinguish between our five senses and the mental faculties described in the previous page. The five sense organs, i.e., sight, sound, touch, smell, and taste, are mere extensions of the body which help us connect to the environment. But the mental faculties are the non-physical or spiritual gifts that help us create and shape our environment. The difference between man and other living things, like, say, our pets, is that while animals operate from mostly sense organs, they blend with their environment. But Man can use his mental faculties to create and recreate his Environment. Sense organs help us to absorb information from the environment, while faculties help us to translate it into meaningful creations. Therefore it is vitally important to choose and absorb information aligned with our worthy ideal resulting in creating value for yourself and those around you.

As James Allen rightly stated in his book As a Man Thinketh published in 1906: "*Mind is the master power that molds and makes, and man is mind, and evermore he takes the tool of thought, and, shaping what he wills brings forth a thousand joys, a thousand ills. He thinks in secret, and it comes to pass. Environment is but a looking glass.*"

Everybody is anxious to change and improve their circumstances but unwilling to improve themselves or their thought process – also called beliefs. They remain tied up to their own habits and thoughts like a slave, blaming external circumstances for not being able to progress. So, the obvious questions would be:

- What exactly is causing unwillingness to improve or change?
- If at all something must change, what should be the starting point?
- How does one know which change or altered state will move him forward or backward in the success journey?

To answer these questions, one must understand the importance of self-awareness, also known as Knowing Thyself. The first step to making a significant change in life is to change the picture and beliefs that we hold of ourselves, i.e., Self-image. Let's explore this further in Chapter 3.

Chapter 3
Self-Image and Attitude

Self-Image is the picture you hold in your mind about yourself. It is what you think you are and what you think you are capable of, such as how much you can earn, how confident you are, and so on. It is a blueprint of how one should live and varies from person to person. It constitutes the SumTotal of beliefs you hold about yourself and your lifestyle. Unfortunately, often, these beliefs are not even yours; these are ideas and perceptions formed based on other people's opinions about you – your teachers, parents, friends, colleagues, and bosses, and many of these beliefs are established in early childhood. These beliefs and opinions are also known as paradigms and are very hard to change. But unless they change, the results in your life will never change. Let's see why the paradigms are so hard to change.

The concept of Psycho-Cybernetics in humans was introduced and explained by Dr. Maxwell Maltz in his famous book Psycho-Cybernetics. It is a natural scientific mechanism built in humans and even animals. We are aware of and apply this concept to multiple machines and devices. The airplane flies on a cybernetics mechanism. While enroute from Dubai to Paris, when there is weather turbulence, the airplane deviates off track. The cybernetics mechanism in the construct will send a message to the traffic control, and the airplane will automatically be brought back on the right track. This is how the whole journey of several hours is covered safely – by repeated corrections several times before the flight lands at the right destination.

This is a natural law, just like the law of gravity and the law of electricity, and applies to our human minds. It helps us to stay focused and maintain order in our lives. It works on our beliefs and paradigms. The actions that we perform daily are driven by those sets of paradigms.

Paradigms do not exist in the conscious mind; they exist in the subconscious mind. Based on scientific research, we already know that there are two minds – the *conscious* and the *subconscious*. The conscious mind can think, reason, imagine, and will, but the subconscious mind can only receive anything that is impressed upon it emotionally. Once impressed, it becomes a command, and the cybernetics mechanism ensures that you follow the actions required to manifest that belief or idea forever unless you produce a new Y idea to overwrite the old X idea. The body is just an animal of habit, and it performs actions based on instructions received from preset programming in the subconscious mind. Sometimes, we do not even remember locking the front door when leaving the house; we may have done it simply by habit.

However, this cybernetics mechanism is impersonal and does not understand the difference between positive and negative; it does not understand whether certain action you undertake is intended to be good or bad. The law just operates 24X7. Therefore, if you are not getting the actual results that you genuinely want, then there must be some fundamental change in one or more of your beliefs that will then result in a change in actions and hence results. For example, while mentoring the Insurance sales folks, personal development coach Bob Procter asked them to change one simple habit, i.e., showing up at 9 am in the office every morning to call prospective clients. By the end of that year, the company's profit jumped by millions of dollars across America. To give my own example, simply by changing one habit of replacing the first intake in the morning, which was coffee, with a glass of warm water, I could significantly revers a certain long-term nagging health issue.

The book Psycho-Cybernetics gives several examples of transformed lives just because the students were hypnotized to believe that they could do what they earlier thought they could never accomplish. If, in childhood, a person of authority, such as a parent or teacher, said that your Math is poor, you would tend to believe it wholeheartedly and lead your entire life, school, college, career decision, and business profile, and so on based on that one belief. We nurture hundreds of such beliefs based on which we make life choices and take action. So then, what steps should one take to amend one's self-image? First, buy yourself a new notebook or, if you like, a fancy journal.

Step 1: Knowing thyself – the first step, of course, is to be aware and know your worthy ideal, as explained in chapters 1 and 2 of this book. Analyze for what you are here. Take your time on this. If you do not find an answer immediately, no worries, keep doing your current work, the answer will automatically and suddenly surface with utmost clarity sooner or later, simply because you are seeking it now.

Step 2: List down your significant paradigms - all of them – positive and negative ones, on a sheet of paper, one after the other. Examples of your beliefs could be such as: (1) I am not qualified enough for that position, (2) My business is too small to make an international footprint, (3) I am not a good cook, (4) I have a beautiful body (5) I am quite confident and know it all in my field (6) I am really fat …

Step 3. Match the paradigms or beliefs that support your worthy ideal. Tick them and place a cross next to the beliefs that are not in favor of your worthy ideal. Let us see one example of this step:

If your worthy ideal is to be a successful Art Coach, then an example of a supporting paradigm would be: *My teaching skills are very good, and I am improving every day.* An example of a bad paradigm for this ideal would be: *I am not good enough to start my coaching business.*

Sometimes it may be difficult to identify if a certain belief is good or not. By looking at your unwanted behavior, you can identify negative beliefs so you can disapprove and swap them for a better one. Ask yourself these questions –

- What beliefs support this action?
- Why do I believe this?
- Is this belief based on facts or assumptions or a false conclusion?
- Is there any rational reason for such a belief?
- Could it be that I am mistaken in this belief?
- Would I come to the same conclusion as some other person in a similar situation?
- Why should I continue to function as if this was true if there is no real reason to believe this?

Review the unwanted belief from all angles. This method will surely give impressive results because whatever your reality is, it is based on your belief. If your belief changes, your reality also will.

Step 4. Rationally falsify and replace the negative beliefs one by one with new positive beliefs. When you repeatedly review and think about the new belief, the old one will gradually fade away. The new beliefs will metamorphosize into a new paradigm. If you start believing that b*y the end of this year, you can easily have 50-100 customers,* your intention will trigger movements in the Universe to bring forth people and ideas in this direction, enabling the body to start automatically taking action as needed. That's how businesses grow. There is nothing happening by force; you let things come to you by changing your self-image.

Let me give an example from my own life. Other than my full-time employment, I have a side hustle of conducting craft workshops through which I spread awareness about upcycling art, teaching to as many people as possible. Initially, I was not sure this could turn into a profitable business. But the moment I decided to become an entrepreneur and bought myself the license, there was a significant paradigm shift. I naturally started attracting new business. I had to change some ideas and thought processes to get to where I am today. One thing led to another; not only am I successful as a craft coach, but I am also a successful inspirational researcher and writer and have started my next business as a personal development and laws of life awareness coach.

Step 5. To change paradigms by imaging or visualization: The mind does not know the difference between mental imagery and physical experience. It triggers the same feelings as if they were real. The subconscious mind registers only visuals (real or imagined) supported by strong feelings. Therefore, it is vitally important to think of positive imagery aligned with your worthy ideal. You must hold on to this despite extremely opposing data feeds from the external world, such as news, friends, or anyone not in favor of the worthy ideal. This is an immensely powerful technique to change paradigms. By making the thought visuals consistent with the worthy ideal, you are creating new connections and a new blueprint for better and bigger results. *Remember, no person and no circumstance on earth can prevent you from improving your self-image. The degree to which you improve the image yourself will be in exact proportion to the amount of truth that you can honestly accept and the amount of positive change you put into engineering your new self-image – the New You –* from PGI Seminars.

Understanding the psychology of the self can mean the difference between success and failure, love and hate, bitterness and happiness. The discovery of the real self can rescue a crumbling marriage, recreate a faltering career, and transform victims of personality failure. On another plane, discovering yourself means the difference between freedom and compulsions of conformity.' – Maxwell Maltz

> ***You will become as small as your controlling desire, as great as your dominant aspiration- James Allen.***

Now, there is another important aspect driving personal development along with Self Image - the secret word: Attitude. Attitude is a composite of Thoughts, Feelings, and Actions. Your attitude is everything about you; in fact, it is the expression of your self-image. Not just thoughts, not just feelings, not just actions, the sum of it. The only way you can improve the results in your life is to take full responsibility for your attitude.

Attitude may be of two types – your attitude toward yourself and your attitude toward others. The shape of your life is determined by your attitude toward yourself. This is an area that we can learn to control. People with the best attitude just naturally rise to the top. They are aware of their strengths and make the best use of them. It's not that they are luckier than others.

Your attitudes towards everything will automatically change when you change your self-image. You have a good attitude when your thoughts, feelings, and action are all aligned. Your attitude will appear to be bad when there is a mismatch between any one of the three components. Let us understand this with an illustration first and then with an example.

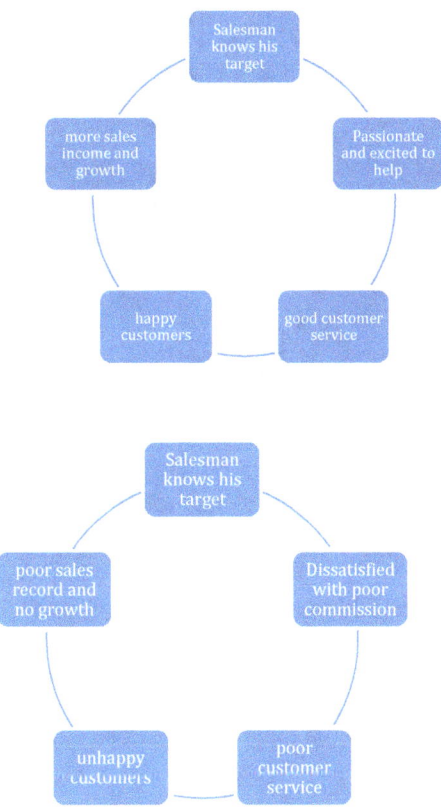

In the two scenarios shown above, which are set in the same environment, the attitude towards the service is the main differentiating factor. The first salesperson is very enthusiastic about achieving his target. He takes all actions to provide the best service to clients, which results in more sales and delighted customers. This salesperson's action is driven by internal passion and not by external rewards, salary, or commission. In the second scenario, the salesperson, even though he knows his target, remembers his poor commission instead of thinking about how to serve the customer better. This puts him in low emotional feelings and lowers his enthusiasm resulting in inaction and poor customer service. This repeats like a vicious circle and explains why one person progresses quickly and others remain the same even after several years. There is a very well-known quote for this:

Attitude determines Altitude.

The greatest discovery of my generation is that human beings can alter their lives by altering their attitude of minds.

– Willian James

Not just individuals but also large companies, organizations, and entities such as sports clubs can apply these principles and train their staff to maintain a cheerful outlook towards themselves and others. Ideally, any change in an organization should commence with changes in the attitude of the members for it to enable effective transformation in the work environment.

How can one change the self-image and improve the attitude? Just like Nature has a process for every creation, we need to have a clear Roadmap to follow the self-image transformation. We need a clear Goal. Let us explore this further in Chapter 4.

Chapter 4
Vision, Goal, and Purpose

The latest measurements with the Hubble Space Telescope, as recent as 2021, suggest the Universe is expanding faster than scientists' predictions. The Universal Intelligence is expanding along with it. We, being the creation of the same Universe, should also grow and evolve continuously. That is absolutely a Law. It is this desire that reflects inside of us as a constant longing and discontent throughout life. The voice of the creative power inside us speaks all the time through signs, symbols, and feelings. We tend to either ignore and suppress it, or we try to manage this desire by seeking joy outside of ourselves, such as immersing ourselves in filler activities like excessive shopping, eating, or entertaining in so many ways. Still, never get the happiness that we seek.

While the Law requires us to expand continuously, the program and plan to do so also was made available inside every living thing. It exists in the Universal Intelligence inside and outside of us. This is both efficient and effective work of the Supreme Intelligence. The work of creation does not happen every day; it is on auto pilot. Birds know when and how to mate and build nests, tigers tend to their cubs and hunt ferociously, and dogs have a heightened sense of smell…. Human beings, however, have the additional gift of the mental faculties to connect to the Universal intelligence to create, grow, and progress, constantly raising the awareness level. This is over and above the basic ability to produce offspring like birds and animals. Hence, to align with the Law of Life, it is not just the responsibility of a certain set of people in society, but each and every human being's responsibility.

The only sure and certain way for expansion is by planning. No one knows yet how far we can get, but at least we must try. If one argues that it is not our responsibility to be part of this study, that it is enough for man to be born, eat, reproduce, and die, my view would be that they are wasting human life; they might as well have been born as a cat, a pig, or a deer if basic survival is what they are looking for. Humans can be much more than this. We must thrive, not just survive. This is exactly what is expected of us - it would be a sin to refuse to participate and contribute. It would be like non-confirming your own basic right – the right to being rich, the right to live big and better, the right to be successful.

If you put the acorn in your pocket, it will die in some days. If you plant it in fertile soil in warm sunlight and water it regularly, in some years, it turns into an oak tree. Similarly, if you have an idea, you need the plan to take it forward. The first step is to set a target, even if a short-term one. Unless you have a certain target, you won't know which direction to move. Unless a ship has a destination, there is no value for the captain's knowledge as he cannot use it. The same goes for the journey of life. For us to ensure we participate in the progress one way or another, we, too, need a clear path.

The intention here is not to say that every man, woman, or person must become a scientist, engineer, or researcher. The value added to our progress can be served in infinite ways. Our society is well-structured to follow the pattern to a great extent. We need nursery teachers, nurses, bus drivers, masons, painters, and farmers, and they are all playing an indirect role in man's progress. Everyone is adding value in their own way. But the question here is, are they doing it as a burden or a responsibility? If everyone wears the thinking hats, putting focus and effort into doing their work to the fullest possible potential, then there will be faster and more productive progress – people will be happier, healthier, and more successful. There are three components to the roadmap, as follows: *Vision, Goal, and Purpose.*

Let us make it interesting with this story. Dr. Viktor Frankl was an Austrian Psychologist who coined the term logotherapy based on his belief that the search for meaning, even amidst suffering, can constitute a potential solution to human suffering. Dr. Viktor himself was subject to extreme torture for about three years in the German concentration camp. However, he survived it, emerged from the pain and suffering, continued his research, and wrote the incredibly famous book – *Man's search for meaning*. He believed that while a person may be held confined to a room or prison, no one can take away from him the freedom of thought. He said,

"Everything can be taken from a man, but one thing: the last of the human freedoms – to choose one's attitude in any given circumstances, to choose one's own way."

"Finding meaning or the will to meaning is the primary motivation for living. The meaning that an individual finds is unique to each person and can be fulfilled only by that person. Frankl emphasized that the true meaning of each person's life is something that must be discovered by activity in the world through interaction with others, not solely through introspection. Challenging a person with a potential meaning to fulfill evokes the will to meaning." (Graber, 2004, p. 65). This is where *Purpose* comes in.

Each of us has a specific purpose for being here on earth and will eventually figure it out. Society, by default, is structured in a way that every one of us has a certain job to do, but 95 percent of the population think that they take up jobs to earn money or some kind of power and prestige. But be aware that each one picks up a profession, job, or responsibility to find the true meaning of life. People really do not put enough thought into it. This explains why sometimes, even a handsome salary or income from their profession may not fill the discontent or void the person feels in spirit. Everyone should consciously endeavor to find their true purpose. How does one identify the true purpose? The easiest and surest way to figure this out is just by asking two simple questions:

1. Does this activity/job/service/business make you happy? Do you absolutely enjoy this activity?

2. Does this help and benefit you and others directly or indirectly? Directly such as scientific research and invention, and indirectly such as supporting the direct contributors like teachers, chefs, and entertainers. Different kinds of people like different activities where their soul finds happiness. There is also another set of contributors who have specific agendas like saving the earth, the Red Cross, motivational speakers, Army. They, too, are significant contributors to man's progress.

Once the purpose is truly clear, all we need to do is to weave it into daily life. How to do this? By creating a long-term vision - a vision board. This would be a picture in your mind of what the world will look like with your contribution, result, or at least an interim one. Of course, it will include what you would look like after achieving your dream.

One of the finest examples of visioneering can be witnessed in this beautiful country - The United Arab Emirates, founded by HH Shk Zayed, fondly remembered as the father of this nation. It's an example to show Heaven can be created on earth too! In just a span of 50 years, between 1972 to 2022, the rulers of the country have completely transformed UAE's landscape from a cluster of pearl fishing villages to a global powerhouse. It is today one of the world's primary attractions in all aspects – Investment, Tourism, Art, Literature & Culture, Scientific and astronautical advancement, Artificial intelligence, and more.

Pictured here is one of the world's most beautiful architecture – the Museum of Future located in Dubai, United Arab Emirates. The Museum of the Future welcomes people of all ages to see, touch, and shape our shared future - go on a journey through futures and bring hope and knowledge back to the present. It gives glimpse of how the world – what society, technology, transport, airspace would look like 50 years from now i.e., in 2072.

Creating an image using the power of imagination is called Visioneering. This is the same core principle or steps from which all inventions stemmed. Einstein confirmed the same point as well. He stated that:

> *"Imagination is everything. It is the preview of life's coming attractions." – Albert Einstein*

So, we can say that the purpose is the *Why* in your life that makes you get up every morning and go to work. Your vision is the *What* – the Destination, the final or interim result that you are looking to achieve. The result could be anything, like a set of bright students for a teacher, happy and healed patients for a doctor, advanced technology and new inventions, advanced health and nutrition solution, renowned influence, or just about anything as per your chosen field that makes you happy.

However, between the purpose and the desired result, there is a big gap, which is *the How*. How can one get the result? What are the steps needed? This can be achieved through the *Goal setting process*. While the purpose and Vision could be one only, Goals may be innumerable, short, and long terms goals. Goals are intertwined with our everyday lives. Therefore, goals could be personal such as relationships, wealth, well-being, health goals, money, financial growth, professional or career growth, and such steps that will help ease the process of reaching the final vision. For example, a politician's goal could be to win the election so that he can implement his vision for his State. An investment banker or a lawyer's goal could be to become the most sought-after in their field so they can offer the best possible service to their clients, who also, in turn, have their own personal goals and visions. So, we are all interconnected, and goal setting becomes a part of the social fabric down to the family level.

As Bob Procter puts it: *A proper goal will give you the necessary incentive to grow in Awareness.* You are presently a perfect expression of infinite power because of your consciousness, awareness, and ability to think. The goal will help you to direct the power in the right manner to live your purpose to attain true happiness and satisfaction. As you become more consciously aware of your oneness with this infinite power within you and its laws of expression, that awareness will be reflected in your results as well. You will be rewarded accordingly, and hence your financial and social status will accordingly progress. Every aspect of your life is, in fact, a mirror reflection of your own level of Awareness. There is a fine point that I do not want the readers to miss. Impressive results could mean social and financial abundance - such as position, power, and money for you personally; however, it may not be that stereotyped in all instances. It depends on the nature of your purpose. It may not necessarily be in the format of personally owned material wealth and riches. Going back to the same example of Mother Theresa, because of her contribution and selfless service, she developed the authority to walk into any large organization and ask for money, i.e., donations, and they will give without asking any questions. That is abundance too!

To ensure a better quality of life, the goal must be chosen as something really special to you. It should be something that you truly desire and that attracts you. It may be a house, a relationship, a certain amount of money, a business deal, a journey, a sports achievement, or anything. It must be important for you and does not need to justify it to anyone. The only condition is that it must serve its purpose; it must be something YOU really want. Not something that your parents want, your spouse wants, or your friends want for you, but something that you want to do, give and serve to yourself and others. And what about if you are in the 50s, the 60s, or 70s? Is that the right time to set a goal? Surely it is. You can start from wherever you are right now. Goal setting is never limited by age.

As your goal is your personal matter and you do not need to explain this or share this with anyone – hence it may be the most bizarre one – this is called TYPE C goal; it may be impossible to achieve, or at least people around you may think so. A Type C goal is one that is not something you *know* you can do or something you *think* you can do; it is something that you want badly enough and does not know how to achieve. That is an absolute challenge - but still, you may be attracted to it like crazy. Go ahead and set your Type C goal. You do not have to worry about how this will manifest – all you need to do is to ensure you truly desire it, envision it, and focus all your energy and life on working towards doing what it takes to achieve this goal. Divert all your thought energy and resources towards the same goal. If you want to make progress on your goals, you must keep at them. This means taking small steps every day to move in the right direction. By accruing small daily victories, you help get the momentum started and keep it going. It may be simple, but not always easy. However, since it is something that you absolutely and genuinely want, you will keep going till you achieve it. To maintain social, mental, and financial balance, goals may change from time to time, but they are all directed always toward your worthy ideal, your purpose, and your final vision. When the goal is achieved, you move to the next one.

Sometimes, goals may involve others around you. It may be a spouse or a group of young entrepreneurs, a group of mountain climbers, a group of students who are working on a common project, or scientists finalizing the launch of an invention. In such a situation, you have the added advantage of mutual help. Support and the additional responsibility of pushing one another to achieve the common goal. Therefore, to be able to really lead a meaningful and accomplished life, finding your true purpose and having an unclouded vision and goal setting is vitally important.

> *Chance favors the prepared mind – Louise Pasteur*

Chapter 5
Your Frequency

In the second chapter on Awareness, we saw a little structural illustration to understand the relation between Thought energy and how it manifests into Results. In this chapter, we shall delve deeper into thoughts and feelings that determine your frequency which in turn affect the results in your life.

Source: Procter Gallagher Institute of Personal Development

How are you feeling at this moment? Happy, tired, excited, stressed? Whatever it is, please know that your feeling is vitally important as it is the key that shapes your life. Every minute you create and change the results in your life because of your feelings, most of the time unknowingly. Let me explain this.

As stated earlier, our body is nothing but a mass of molecules vibrating at a very high frequency. If you put a buzzing bee under the microscope, you will see a bunch of molecules. However, a bee can operate only on one frequency; it can only be a bee as long as it lives. Everything vibrates, and vibration indicates the state of being – whether dead or alive. But man, is the highest form of God's creation. In our case, Frequency would not mean being in a state of survival, unlike animals. It indicates the energetic quality of a person. Frequency can be sensed intuitively - you can tell a person's energy when they walk into a room; for example, some people draw you closer, and others make you want to keep a distance. You feel good when you see a newborn baby smiling; you feel sad when watching destructive news on the television. As humans, you can create anything you want simply by managing your frequency, unlike other creatures. If you think about something in your mind, you can hold it in your hands too. This is how everything was created. Why, then, do a small population of people live a phenomenally successful and affluent life, a vast majority have a mediocre life, and another group live in constant lack, limitation, and struggle every day?

There are certain laws that one must follow to maneuver the frequencies. If you want to call someone in Kuala Lumpur, you will dial their phone number and can immediately connect; if you change even one digit, it will not work. If you want to listen to FM Radio, you cannot tune into AM Radio; you must tune into FM only to go to that frequency manually. We can also call it the Frequency principle or law, and it operates in our lives in a certain way. On one side, life energy is flowing to and through us, and on another side, there are infinite levels of frequency. Everything you want is sitting on different frequencies. The current results determine what frequency you are on right now. If you want, let's say, a promotion, you have to channelize your life energy towards doing and giving your best, attaining mastery at what you do. How do you do that?

By generating emotions as if you have been promoted already. That is becoming the person you want to be.

The feeling is the medium that you need to be able to jump from one frequency to other. How can you get a good feeling when your current results are not favorable? Is it even possible? Yes. Absolutely possible. By shifting your thoughts, you can change your feeling and hence the frequency. By thinking - using your imagination, you can imagine in your mind the situations and things you would do when in that new state. The feeling is the language your subconscious mind understands. It is the signal and will give an indication to the subconscious mind about your new end state, which controls the actions that you do. The subconscious mind will hence lead you to behave in a manner as if you have already reached the end state.

Who is stopping you? Imagine anything you want. No one can see it. The subconscious mind does not understand the difference between reality and imagination; that is why you cry when you watch a movie. When you focus your mind and imagine the good happening to you, the good feeling carries you up to that frequency where you will receive what you desire. All the plots, plans, people, and resources needed to manifest the change is riding on that frequency. The subconscious mind has a way of connecting to the universal intelligence once it receives a signal from feelings. The Universal Intelligence then finds a way to manifest and attract the things as desired into the person's life. The importance of feelings was explained intelligently by Neville Goddard in his books and speeches. He has explained this with his interpretations of the Bible, and he went further on to say how the scriptures are not a historical record of the life of the characters such as Jesus and Krishna, but the characters in it are the various states of mind. The scriptures help us to see the wisdom inside of us. When we channelize the thought energy by imagination and visioneering in the direction we want to, then our world tends to shape in the same way. Simply put, wherever our attention goes, that is what we become. It is important, therefore, to be in a higher frequency for a prolonged period to achieve the desired goal. There are infinite levels of frequency. The highest level of frequency is divine intelligence, eternal bliss when you become one with the universal energy, and the lowest is death when your body does not vibrate anymore. I suspect this is what Albert Einstein exactly meant when he said:

"Everything is energy, and that's all there is to it. Match the frequency of the reality you want, and you cannot help but get that reality. It can be no other way. This is not philosophy; this is physics."

The well-being and success stated above are not just relevant to financial status, projects, achievements, and external results. The principles apply to the body and health matters too. In recent years, Doctor Joe Dispenza conducted innumerable analyses and research work. Some of the thoughts from his books and speeches are also summarised below:

Thoughts create emotions. Thought is the language of the mind, and emotion is the language of the heart. The heart is the pumping station; based on the kind of emotion the thought is feeding into the heart, the heart sends the signals to the genes in the body. The genes in the body contain the intelligence to tell the body what to do. The formula and the direction come from the genes, so really, every cell of your body is your mind, and your mind is not a separate object. It is the omnipresent and ever-expanding universal intelligence, and it is connected to every cell in the body. So, for example, if you are thinking of an old memory that is hurtful and painful, it's going to trigger either sadness or guilt, or you may have happy memories of your childhood days. The feelings will pass on to all the cells in the body through the heart, which will up-regulate or down-regulate genes, thereby either creating disease for the body or healing it. When you are stressed, in order to protect yourself, the Universal Intelligence may create a situation where you lose your job or you will develop a new disease. The Universal Intelligence thinks differently than us; it does not give the same meaning that we give to things. It simply sees this as cause and effect. Based on various studies conducted, I have created an analogy of this concept as follows:

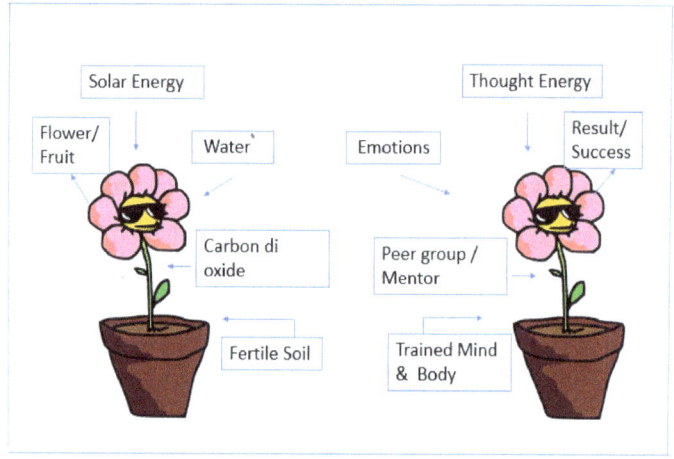

Therefore, your only task under any given circumstances is to feel emotionally good. There is no direct way to change the results; one cannot influence it directly – it will follow the process as per universal intelligence and its pattern plan. This has been very beautifully stated in the **Verse 2.47** of the *Bhagavat Gita*: It states that you have a right to perform your prescribed duties, but you are not entitled to the fruits of your actions. Never consider yourself to be a cause of the results of your activities, nor be attached to inaction.

> *karmaṇy-evādhikāras te mā phaleṣhu kadāchana*
> *mā karma-phala-hetur bhūr mā te saṅgo 'stvakarmaṇi*

This really means your job is to feel good – give it your all and live the process. It is up to the universal intelligence to create and manifest the results. You will not be able to control the results but can control your feelings and action through which the results will automatically manifest. So, your only task is to be the best and feel the best believing in the Universal process. The chapter on Believing later in the book will clarify further on this.

Imagination is an immensely powerful mental faculty that can be used to regulate your emotions. Even though your circumstances may be against you, you can still generate positive emotions by using your imagination – let's say you want to crack a big business deal. You will have to do this exercise – lie down or sit in a relaxed state, almost about to fall asleep, and imagine the scene and hold inner conversations between yourself and related parties as if you already got the deal that your partners, colleagues, and friends are congratulating you, you have a large financial gain currently, buying a new car or whatever. Whatever you think, your emotions align with that. Because they are connected, it will be a matter of time only then when the images picturized will soon materialize. The only condition is that you must feel and become part of the vision imagined. I have practiced this, and it has worked out so well for me; more importantly, in some cases, the manifestation happened a lot earlier than I wished. Absolute magic!

To some readers, this practice may appear weird, but being a big fan and follower of this concept, I want to assure the readers that the above actually works. The most popular real-life proof of this is how people normally materialize love and marriage. When you are in love with someone, their image, your imaginary conversations, and romantic interactions keep playing in your imaginary future all the time, everywhere you go and whatever you are doing. In most instances, constant visualization with strong emotions manifests the romantic partner. Since you have chosen the person already, the vision is very clear – the specifics are clear, and the message is received clearly by the Universe. The same principle may be applied to materialize everything else in life too.

A few popular and effective ways to raise vibrational frequency are as follows:

Gratitude – this is one of the easiest ways to quickly raise your vibration. This can be tested instantly; you can stop reading and look at all things around you in the room, wherever you are sitting. There are hundreds of things to be thankful for. More significantly, you are alive and have access to universal energy and intelligence one more day on this earth – that is, today. What a miracle! What a beautiful thing to be happy and feel good about. When you feel low, try applying this simple technique. The power of gratitude is explained in more detail in a later chapter.

Love – Another straightforward way to instantly feel good is to recall someone or something you love, whether it is your mother or grandfather, your pet, your spouse, or a mentor teacher from childhood. Love is one of the highest vibrating states of being and can even pull you out of hell. The thought will instantly make you feel lighter, happier, and relaxed.

Generosity – Man's true purpose and spiritual character is in creating and giving. Nothing on this earth can make you feel happier than the fulfilment that you get when you are able to give and help someone. You feel proud; you feel accomplished; you feel full, and your heart swells up – in fact, you feel powerful. Giving generates happiness from the inside out, not sourced from outside of you. So, this has a long-lasting effect.

Meditation – It feels great when one can bring their attention to the present. Practicing the art of being present liberates you from the clutches of traumatic thoughts of the past or fearful future – it keeps you stabilized and aligns with the larger truth, the actual inner being. This may be practiced by breath work and meditative techniques taught by your mentor or guru. I personally believe that when you are giving your 100% attention to anything, you are being fully present, and that is as good as meditation – for example, if you are in a performing art class or learning fine arts, or working on a research paper, you are providing your undivided attention and being present with that activity. This is something that has personally worked for me very well. But again, depending upon the teacher-student connection, one can see what works best for them.

Detoxing the body and lifestyle habits such as nutritious food, good music, and books also play a vital role in feeling good or bad. Everything we put into the body is *Prana* or life force energy, whether it be fruits, meat, alcohol, TV, books, or music. Consuming dead energy like processed or fried food will lower the vibration while eating natural and organic food will lighten and keep the absorption process in good form. Alcohol beyond a limited quantity is found to function as a depressant. It is important to be selective about the media intake as well; take only information aligned with your goal and purpose rather than data that would pull you away from your purpose and make you feel good.

In most cases, good physical outdoor exercise, traveling, simple walking and a good night's sleep will also immensely raise your vibration. Every time you walk out of the gym or after a physical exercise, don't you get the refreshed and powerful feeling of being light and joyful? Physical activities give you a good night's sleep as well. My husband's eyesight got significantly corrected in his early fifties when he started following early to bed routine against erratic late nights in his younger days.

Your surroundings and peer groups play a critical role as well in how you feel. Make your surrounding as beautiful and pleasant as you would like. You do not need to spend a fortune on this, but simple things such as plants around the house and good lighting can instantly change the vibrations in a room. Do not surround yourself with depressing and negative people who always talk about failures, lack, limitations, and how life has been cruel to them. Instead, connect and network with people who have common goals and purposes in your preferred field and passion. This will keep you motivated and in good vibes. Being in a high vibration will really enable you to be the best version of yourself, so you can do more, be more and give more - do justice to the expansion-seeking spirit inside of you. That is the secret to a blissful and fulfilled life!

Chapter 6
Laws of the Universe

As stated earlier, everything in the world has a pattern plan designed by universal intelligence. If one gets an understanding of the calculations, characteristics, and workings of these things, then nature's models can be recreated for the benefit and progress of humanity. Although most of the universal intelligence is still beyond human comprehension, we have made considerable progress in some areas. When we learned about the laws of motion and laws of gravity, it became easier to build complex architecture and machineries. Similarly, when we understood how sound and radio waves travel and how they can be captured, the first radio was designed. The airplanes, rockets to the moon, spaceships, missiles, medicines, motors, and microphones; in each field, man poured in decades of research and worked on these laws for the benefit of humankind.

Let us take the simple example of electricity. Man did not create this energy – as Einstein said, Energy cannot be created or destroyed. Only in the last 100 years or so have we learned how to harness this energy to design electrical appliances that we use in everyday life by studying the nature of electricity, conductors, insulators, etc. Similarly, Thought being a form of energy, it is important to channelize the thought energy in a certain manner to be able to lead a more productive and successful life.

The Laws of Life were first properly analyzed and documented by Sir Raymond Holliwell. There are, of course, dozens of laws for different fields or aspects of life, but primarily we can refer to eleven significant laws of which one must, at a minimum, be aware of. These have been explained in the following pages:

Law of Thinking

To the average person in society, life is a complex, mysterious, and unpredictable journey. The future is a fearful demon, and tomorrow is an uncertain expedition. But it will be a lot simpler if one holds the key. If a thing appears mysterious, it is because we do not know enough about it, so the key is really *Understanding*; if we endeavor to understand how and why things operate, then it will be easier to maneuver life to our advantage and achieve desired results.

As specified earlier, Thought is a potent energy that can transcend all times and space at once. It is an unlimited force. True progress and the evolution of humanity are only possible if this energy is really put to proper use. Our thought process and resulting mental state are primarily responsible for the events unfolding in this life.

We are constantly thinking. What we think keeps changing, but we cannot stop thinking. It flows through us constantly like the air we breathe. We can direct this thought energy into constructive channels of expression. When our thoughts are aimless and imperfect, we create pain and confusion for ourselves. Focused thought like that of a scientist, performing artists, surgeons, teachers, students, and sportsmen will help in producing a constructive and beneficial product or service which has great value in it.

Most of us mistake mental activities for thoughts. If you are thinking about a disturbing past incident and feeling those emotions now, that is not real thinking; it's re-living the past and not considered productive or progress-oriented thinking. It only wastes your present time and generates a negative mental and physical influence on your health and well-being. If you are thinking about a future potential fearful situation and negative conversations or consequences, that too is not real thinking; it's just a mental activity called worry or fear and adds absolutely no value to your future results. Only focused and consistent thought arising from the study and understanding of a subject or a problem would produce positive results in life. So, one must make learning and studying a lifelong activity.

Law of Supply

All of us want to get better and bigger in whatever we do. We want more money, a bigger house, a promotion, and business expansion, among other things. There is absolutely nothing wrong with wanting more, as God originally desired for us to grow and develop. It is because we are not satisfied with the current result that we work on new inventions and new technological development to get better, more comfortable, and more efficient. The age-old paradigm that one should be satisfied with what they have and be happy with little does not really help us because this is against nature's law and hence may cause conflict in the body leading to ill health.

The universe itself is perpetually expanding, and hence it is only natural that we evolve with it as it grows. There is plenty everywhere for all of us. While money is Man's currency and is limited, God's currency is ideas, which is unlimited, so if one has less money, it does not mean there is any less abundance in their life. They can withdraw great ideas and worthy ideal from the Universal intelligence that constantly talk to us – ideas are free and unlimited, unlike bank notes. There is never a need to worry or fear about losing out in competition, whether it is a service or business, because they are not limited by money but unlimited by ideas.

Worrying restricts and limits the supply at hand. All one needs to do is apply focused thinking and work on their ideas and purpose, aiming to provide better service or product. This understanding will help to feel abundant and keep the thoughts focused on creative living, which will eventually lead to more prosperity and well-being.

Law of Attraction

This is the most popular, most sought after, but very less understood law. To desire is to expect, and to expect is to achieve. After understanding the law of supply as stated above and knowing that everything is abundant around us, the next step should be to acknowledge the Desires (or ideas) that arise within us and then to expect that they will manifest for the simple reason that no desire will be planted in your heart until it is already yours – meaning the end state that you desire is already existing, you will have to reach that frequency to be able to see the result in physical form. How do you move to that frequency?

Abraham Hicks states – ***As you think, you vibrate. As you vibrate, you attract***. This is about the principle of how frequency operates. This concept was rightly and brilliantly summed by James Allen as follows: "As a Man thinketh in his heart so is he." Simply put, *you become what you think about, and you manifest what you become.*

The law of attraction works in a very intriguing way. It is not as simple as wanting something, imagining, and then manifesting it. The most important criteria are Intention; you need to really intend to do or be something in the spirit, by feeling, by living it to attract what you want in life. What we see around us in physical form is the result of what we are currently thinking. What we intend to get, what we truly desire, already exists at a higher level of frequency where we can see with the inner eye – the eye of imagination – where unlimited possibilities exist. The reality is in that frequency, and we have the choice to live in that elevated frequency.

Therefore, what we need to add to the visualization is the feeling of already being there and the intent to possess it, be it or get it. This is the fundamental logic behind how the law of attraction works. To achieve something which is in the fourth dimension (where time does not exist), you must literally intend to be or get there by believing it is already yours. Let me give a simple example. Joining the Toastmasters community to develop my presentation and leadership skill was on my to-do list for 2022 though I have been contemplating it since early 2021. I had the true intention of being a part of this network and growing with them. However, to my utter surprise, it so happened that one of our mastermind partners whom I met in 2021 was a VP of Education of a toastmaster club in the same town, and he enrolled me within one week of stating my goal to him. So, the goal was achieved several months before due to true intent! In the dimension of true intent, time collapses, and a future event can happen immediately!

Law of Receiving

"Give and it shall be given unto you, good measure running over."

Luke 6.38

This is the simplest of all laws and, if properly understood, will undoubtedly help you transform your life completely. The law requires you to offer something to get back an equal proportion of something in return. You need to give your time, money, energy, and resources into something to get something in return.

You cannot expect to have something for nothing; it does not work like that. In fact, getting should not be the focus at all; **_Getting is the result, the outcome of what you are giving_**. If I spend more and more time writing, I will get better at it and offer more value in my writing, which in turn will attract more readers. It is because of our lack of understanding that we think we must get before giving. It should be clearly understood that giving is the first law or the fundamental law of life and is the first law of creation too. When you desire something, believe it, and achieve the same, you are, in fact, giving something out into the universe.

If you inject fear and worry into that, the law will still work but provide negative results, retard the process of getting even though you may be giving your best as these laws work in harmony. To summarize, we can say: "It is more blessed to give than to receive. As we freely give, we freely receive." One must also make sure that they give where it is good to give and not support an evil cause or to someone who will not help themselves and others. Give to those who desire to improve, grow, and contribute, and it shall be returned manyfold to you.

Law of Increase

This Law is about the act of praising, whether praising God, the Law, or what we desire. Praise has ever been a common method used to get the attention and blessing of God, as per all religions on this planet. Hindus sing Bhajans and Kirtans to praise the lord, and the Hebrews have used it for ages, as per the Bible too. When we praise the lord, our thoughts expand, and the frequency widens to reach larger and better results in life. This makes a change inside of us where we unknowingly gain the blessing.

Praise is a tonic of the mind and magnetizes all good around you. It implies you see good in everything and puts you in a positive mindset, thus maintaining your position on the right frequency. This simple technique is applied by trainers of animals such as dolphins and dogs, where they give a pat and a morsel of food after each act.

Everyone has undergone a situation where their superior or person of authority in their life has criticized them for something; how do you feel? Dejected, demotivated, and feeling like quitting. Praise does the opposite – it motivates, encourages, and pushes you to perform better. It is scientifically proven that even plants respond very well to praise. One must also remember to praise oneself for the work accomplished rather than blame and feel guilty for something that went wrong. Praise changes our observation and perception about life. There is a little trick to it, too – you do not praise only after you receive something. The law can be practiced in advance of receiving something or even in adversities, and this will help to speed up the manifestation process. This is not just a testament but is one of the Laws of the Universe.

Law of Compensation

You may not have heard about such a law before but may have discussed and analyzed it from various aspects. This is about what and how much you earn financially and other benefits as a reward for the efforts you put in.

This is the same as saying – ***You reap as you sow.*** It has been categorically stated in all major religious books, be it the Bible or the Bhagavat Geeta. We see this in most movies, too; the hero gets his reward, and the villain gets his punishment at the end for their behavior. But the question to ask is that – are we getting fair returns for our efforts? Are we happy with the compensation received? Most people *think* they are not. One must understand the law of compensation properly to see what is not working and their miscalculations in getting the desired compensation. The law itself cannot change, but the mistakes can be corrected. There are three fundamental factors that contribute to one's compensation – the **need** for what you offer, your **ability** to do it, and the **difficulty replacing** you.

You cannot expect increasing returns from the same quality of service you have been providing earlier. You need to change something and increase the value of what you deliver. Become the best in what you are doing, learn and improve every day, so much so that it becomes quite difficult to replace you, as there is no end to learning.

Even if they replace you, you are already so good at it that you can start your own business in this line. Similarly, the higher the demand for your service, the more compensation you get. The celebrities like movie stars and top singers performances are demanded across the globe; their work remains unique and best in class. No one can replace them as they themselves become a unique brand by virtue of their performance. You can apply the principle in all fields, be it a chef, a builder, a dress designer, a teacher, or any.

Law of Non-Resistance

Desiring a thing is one thing, while *really being ready to receive* is another. This is the fundamental reason, while there are many talented people in a certain field, only a few are able to shine and carve out a niche for themselves. Of course, this takes time with experience and expertise, but the person must be truly ready to receive all the good with open arms when it really knocks the door. The opportunity, customers, and requests come in disguised forms. Applying the law of non-resistance will make it easier to receive the due compensation and rewards.

The widespread belief that Resistance, as a means of securing peace and harmony is a mistaken and misleading idea. The whole field of Marketing and Salesmanship is about the in-depth study of the law of non-resistance itself. Keeping the shop doors open, staff always available to assist, keeping oneself accessible, appearing pleasant and cheerful with a willingness to serve, following up on queries and complaints systematically, keeping clear books of records send out indications of the intention into the universe, which in turn will attract more opportunity and business.

Similarly, having worry and fear about the desired outcome also puts up resistance against the good coming your way. One needs hundred percent faith and open-mindedness to be able to receive all the good. Faith will be discussed in more detail in the upcoming chapter. The Law of non-resistance is seen everywhere in nature, especially in the water – the life source on this planet. Lord Alfred Tennyson has narrated this very beautifully in his poem **The Brook** – I get elated every time I read this. It has stuck in my head since middle school. This is just a small excerpt from this lovely poem:

> *I chatter over stony ways in little sharps and trebles,*
> *I bubble into eddying bays; I babble on the pebbles.*
>
> *With many a curve my banks I fret, by many a field and fallow,*
> *And many a fairy foreland set, with willow-weed and mallow.*
>
> *I chatter, chatter, as I flow to join the brimming river,*
> *For men may come and men may go, but I go on forever.*

The brook has one sole purpose and aim, which is to eventually and eternally merge with the brimming river. So irrespective of what comes its way, it keeps on flowing, bending, hopping, turning, and swirling as needed. This is the way one should live. Mere external circumstances should not stop you from moving forward toward the desired goal; focused thinking and attention are of utmost importance.

Law of Forgiveness

Forgiving is really a powerful way to be in a good vibration. It has nothing to do with someone or something outside of you; it means absolutely letting go completely abandoning.

Buddhists believe that 'Forgiveness is a practice for removing unhealthy emotions that would otherwise cause harm to our mental well-being.' Every other religion says the same thing.

–"*Forgive and ye shall be forgiven*" – **Luke 6:37**

The beloved Prophet (Peace be upon him) said: "Whoever suffers an injury and forgives (the person responsible), Allah will raise his status to a higher degree and remove one of his sins." Muslims believe that Forgiveness is not an obligation but a virtue. While many think that the holy books and manuscripts are historical records, as Neville Goddard points out, I tend to strongly believe these are more scientific guidelines on how to follow the laws of life. Not following the specific purpose or aim in life is a sin; not sticking to your goal and vision is a sin; not playing your role in giving amply for your worthy ideal is a sin, and these may be considered as working against the law.

All the negative emotions, such as anger, jealousy, and impatience, are as much sinful whether you possess them or someone else holds this against you. Forgiveness involves both forgiving someone for doing you wrong and forgiving oneself for not following the law. Both are equally difficult, for the former inculcates hatred in us and the latter guilt, which are extreme emotions detrimental both to our health and wellbeing. Based on numerous studies, the Emotion code is a powerful method of finding and releasing trapped negative emotions that have been stored in the body.

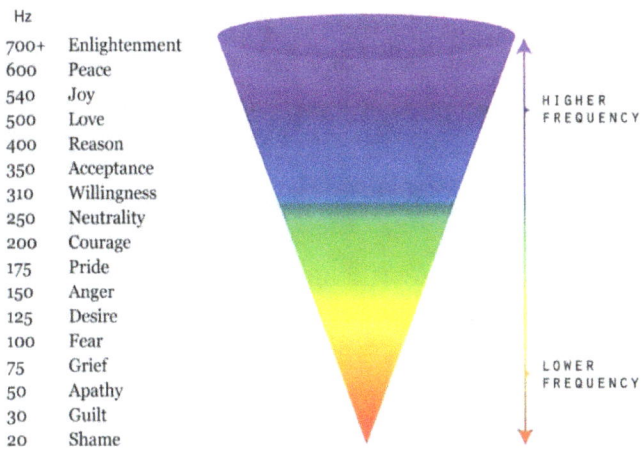

Source: Triad Health Center

Whether it is forgiving yourself or someone else, mentor and coach Mary Morrissey put it very beautifully in her teachings – *Forgiveness is a shift in perception which removes a block in me to my Awareness of love's presence or the power of all that is here.*

Law of Sacrifice

This is my favorite law but, sadly, the most misunderstood Law. People think sacrifice is giving up your own something to benefit others, for example, giving up your food and starving yourself to feed others or giving up your passion, or giving away your money to someone at the cost of your own discomfort or suffering. This is not what sacrifice really means. This is working against the law and actually a sin. This leads to a dissatisfied soul, frustrated and depressed old age ridden with diseases. ***Sacrifice truly means giving up something of a lower value to achieve something of a higher value*** – therefore, entails strict self-discipline to achieve the desired objective.

The best concerts, masterpieces, astronautical advancements, and technological developments could not have been possible without the sacrifice of its contributors. The primary requirement for this law is to have an idea and then discipline oneself to focus all thoughts, attention, and energy towards achieving that goal – not deviating for small pleasures, meaning sacrificing smaller indulgences. This is something we are all already taught from childhood as students; you must give up several hours of watching TV or playing and focus on your studies before the exams in order to achieve a good result. Similarly, when a parent, a teacher, or a coach is focused on bringing well-nurtured, knowledgeable kids, there is a certain amount of time and energy that they put into achieving that desired goal. So, sacrifice is really giving something up of less importance to get something of more priority as per each individual's personal ideals and goals. The results in life, spiritual and material success will be directly proportional to the amount of attention and focus attributed to a certain objective.

Law of Obedience

This is a beautiful Law. The word obey means to submit to the rule or to comply with orders or instructions. As life and thought energies constantly flow through us, we are expected to build and create constantly. All the materials needed to build the life we want are already given to us. In the process of building and receiving the product, there is a certain gestation period, as per the laws of nature.

This is in addition to the laws of the land and government regulations that one must follow: *order is the first principle of any successful system,* and the same is true for our society too. There are two aspects to it, obeying your spirit rather than the conditions around us; that is, the law requires us to be in a creative state. That is, to think of things in existence first by obeying the true inner desires. Then there is obedience to the gestation principle.

People tend to misunderstand that it is God or their fate that is making things happen or delaying them. But as one can observe in nature, a carrot seed takes 14-21 days to sprout, a human baby takes nine months, and a lamb may need five months to be delivered. The cause and effect has its own cycle, and all natural things like plants and animals also pass through these phases of hibernation, breeding, withering, and blooming. If you try to force open the petals of a rosebud, it will soon fall into pieces without blooming fully. That is the law of obedience, and we must respect it fully, so this helps us to manage our expectations and progress toward our goals. Do not give up on yourself or the stakeholders if you do not see the result within a planned time. It will eventually work out – ***consistency and intention are the key***!

Law of Success

'He can who thinks he can.' It is important to understand that God or the Universe wants each one he created to succeed and progress; it is not just for the chosen ones. I want to emphasize here that one should come out of survival mode and start to thrive more, making this world a more contented place. It is not a sin to want more, be more and do more and get more. It is, in fact, a sin to work against the law of life, not to follow the true desire of your soul, and not to serve your purpose.

It would be a sin not to use the mental faculties given to us and stay within the same comfort zone – the known territory.

Everything around us is moving forward, technology, knowledge, awareness, and, more importantly, time. In this scenario, if you do not want to learn more and seek expansion, then it would mean you are really moving backward in time.

A remarkable talent, and higher faculties, are lying dormant in everyone, and it is your responsibility to start developing these for practical use. The law of success is as definite as any other scientific law. So, to apply this law, you must recognize your core strength, worthy ideal, and true passion and *do something* about it. Study, planning, and sacrifice are necessary. Everyone, whether young or old, is entitled to progress. To repeat what we said in the first chapter, Success is the progressive realization of a worthy ideal, in other words bringing oneself and one's actions to a standard higher than the ordinary human standard, being better today than yesterday on a continuous basis.

The most important thing, though, is adopting the core values and systems and having order in place for a methodical approach to progress. There must be a true course, what is just and right, both in thought and action, for it to be truly valuable to humanity and sustainable. That is, we must be righteous, also called *Dharma*. Desire and action without a noble principle will eventually fail and collapse. Success principles may easily be adopted from scriptures or business as they are both akin to scientific guidelines rather than historical narrations. But there is a more fundamental requisite for the law of success and all other laws mentioned above to work, and that is Faith. Let us move on to Chapter 7 and understand this in greater depth.

Chapter 7
Belief & Faith

For a long time, like everyone else – I was of the sense that "**Seeing is Believing**" means that what we see and perceive physically is what we must believe. I was under the impression that reality is what we see with physical eyes around us. But when I started my studies and research on Working with the Law, my perception about *Believing* totally changed. My new awareness about seeing things from the inner eye and using mental faculties such as will and imagination transformed me and raised my awareness level such that I gained new insight as follows:

Believing is Seeing…

Let me explain this remarkably interesting and profound concept step by step with an illustration now. What we perceive as reality is what we see physically happening around us; for example, if the current income of a certain person is 100k annually, he makes his decision, choices, and lifestyle based on what he sees; that is what his current income is. Therefore, he is limited in his belief to the only possible horizon set by his income of 100K annually. On the other hand, if he believes he can earn 100K monthly instead of annually, he will take action proactively to make choices and decisions based on this newly raised financial status which will put him in the frequency of receiving higher income. For him to believe he can earn 100K monthly instead of annually, he must actually see this, imagine this and visualize this with feeling as per the law of vibration and law of attraction explained in the previous chapter. When he starts to research and think about this continuously, his subconscious mind starts seeing new possibilities – from where then two things happen – (1) driven by new ideas and knowledge of possibilities; he will start taking actions and decisions to expand his income, including new habits, new networking, new business deals, new ideas, new career opportunities, advanced delivery quality, and so on and (2) the subconscious mind will start connecting to the universal intelligence to manifest things, to start attracting people, things, circumstances related to the new goal into the life of this person now. This is how he will start raising his financial status to 100k per month. It may take some time, as per the law of gestation, but change is certain. We can see clearly how this works as per the laws explained above.

Imagine (see with an inner eye) →*Believe* → *Manifest*

This is what Seeing *is Believing* originally means and not what we actually see with the external eyes. Hence, we can say believing is actually seeing something transform into reality; it is more futuristic than the current or past state of affairs. Also, this perspective helps us to look at things in a forward-looking manner rather than dwelling on the past or current circumstances to help progress and enthuse the soul.

To believe in the things you can see and touch is no belief at all, but to believe in the unseen is a triumph and a blessing – Abraham Lincoln.

Let us elaborate further on how this works with some more illustrations. Developing a belief is like building a wall or an opaque screen in your mind. Once the wall is laid and consolidated, it becomes a strong barrier or a paradigm. It means it has entered the subconscious mind. This is the scientific working of the mind and not some baseless hypothesis. Belief is closely related to habit, and the body performs actions based on habits. Based on performance, we get results in our life, be it in health, career, financial situation, or any.

That is why it is extremely important to frequently re-look at our beliefs and paradigms, check which ones are progressive and which ones are detrimental, and replace old and redundant beliefs with new thoughts and beliefs - Learning, Unlearning, and Relearning - Unwiring and Rewiring of the brain cells. Relooking at our beliefs is a process to re-align our goals to our definite chief aim or worthy ideal from time to time. We unknowingly develop hundreds of beliefs since childhood, some through our gene memory, some through culture, upbringing, religion, school, peers, and many other sources. Moreover, we would also tend to see things in a certain limited way as it has been fed into our subconscious. Would you really believe in the tooth fairy and gold coin under your pillow now the same way you believed them when you were five? Heightened awareness has now changed your belief, but sadly not in all, and certainly not in the most critical matters in life.

Changing a belief or building a new one is easier said than done. A paradigm can be changed only by one of the two methods:

1) Repeated spaced re-iteration like the TV commercials and, or

2) Sudden strong emotional impact also causes paradigm shifts like a childhood incident – good or bad

It may appear I am repeating a few ideas across different chapters in the book, but rest assured, these are in the right context and definitely emphasize the points in the reader's mind. Using our imagination, will, and focus, we can choose our thoughts and decide to focus our attention on a certain thing repeatedly for a prolonged period transforming it into a belief. I really intend this to be a noticeably big takeaway from this book for the readers.

Going back to the same example, the person who earns 100K per year must start seeing and believing his capability of earning 100K per month. When he builds this new belief, he will be able to effortlessly act and manifest better income over a period of time provided; of course, he follows all the previously mentioned laws. In order to make a decision, he can use the decision chart as summarized

- Is this decision according to the laws of the universe, the law of receiving, compensation, etc.

- Is this decision helping you progress towards your goal

- Does this decision affect anyone or anything adversely,

- If not, please proceed with acting on the new belief and follow the inner intuitive guidance to proceed

The opposite of Decision is Ambivalence - One has to stop being in a state of ambivalence – it means having conflicting thoughts towards the same idea, such as – Shall I do this or not do this, say this or be quiet, give or not give, buy or not buy…Ambivalence is the enemy of Belief. We have to be sure of what we want and decide on having it, being it, or doing it. Once the decision is made, we must convince and discipline ourselves willfully to strengthen the paradigm until it becomes a natural belief. The belief then sets into motion the required action and circumstances to manifest the desire into a reality.

Observe carefully, and you will find everything that happens in daily life is based on your total belief and faith. You believe that your car is still in the parking lot where you left yesterday evening, your office building is still in the same location, and you will find them in the same place;

there is no doubt about it. It is this unshakable knowing that is expected from you for your true passion and desire so that it becomes all yours = you must believe it is already yours. Your attitude will shift to the frequency to manifest it in due course of time.

John 11:26-34- And whosoever liveth and believeth in me shall never die.

The above has been interpreted very beautifully by Neville Goddard as follows – whoever believes in oneself (I referred to as self) shall always progress and never perish. We need to constantly create new beliefs based on new awareness and take actions in line with the belief – this is the only path to progress and success. Just like Christ died and resurrected after a few days – it is a symbolic representation of our old redundant beliefs dying and new beliefs taking their place that will prevent one from perishing. It has been explained beautifully that Christ is the I AM within us, the son, and is the same as the creator. The creation will get invoked only when the belief is upgraded. For it would be a sin to stay in the same old belief and comfort zone without contributing to the expansion and expression of the soul inside. So when Christ dies (that is, when the old idea or belief dies), your sins are erased, making a place for new beliefs and progress. This is also known as the vacuum law of attraction or prosperity. The law applies in the physical world too. Unless you clear your house of old junk, you will not have space for better, nicer new comforts at home. Therefore, it is important to declutter and refresh the house, office, cupboards, and other things periodically. And yes, even the applications in your mobile and mailboxes!

Interestingly, Belief works not just on self but also when we place the belief on someone or something outside of us. Faith is the strong trust and confidence in something or someone, while belief is more to do with the state or habit of mind in which we trust. Having studied the laws of the universe for a while now, and based on my research, I tried to change my belief about eating rice. That consuming rice cause weight gain, and it should be avoided completely from the diet to lose weight – this is a very popular Asian belief, and it never fails to manifest because the public wholeheartedly believes this. I wanted to prove to myself that if I changed my belief around this and still lost weight, it would put my Belief theory to the test. Having decided to lose weight with this new belief, within a short period of time, I came in contact with a popular nutritionist who customizes food and weight loss programs to suit the client's preferences. Within a few weeks, very effortlessly, I lost almost 10 kilos, still eating rice for lunch (though a modified breed of rice – brown instead of white rice). This worked because of my new strong belief and complete faith placed in the nutritionist who promised that the desired result could be achieved soon. When you place trust and faith in another person, whether your coach, mentor, friend, or parent, the burden of worry is taken off of your shoulders, so getting the desired result becomes effortless. We have to simply follow the instructions of the coach/mentor, which is far easier and fun too. There is a popular saying 'When the student is ready, the teacher appears.'

Mathew 17: *Truly I tell you, if you have faith as small as mustard seed, you can say to the mountain, 'Move from here to there', and it will move.* Nothing will be impossible for you. Believing is seeing with the inner eye of imagination that what you desire is already yours. If at all there is a really difficult situation beyond your control, just think of the last line of the classic 'Gone With the Wind,' spoken by Scarlett O'Hara, "After all, tomorrow is another day," and you can renew your belief and faith.

Chapter 8
Fear and Courage

One man with Courage makes a majority

– Andre Jackson

The above statement though short, means a lot. In a herd of hundreds of men who are lost and struggling, if one man rises and provides faith and guidance, there is a tendency to follow the man, and he naturally becomes their leader. Faith and Courage are the foremost characteristics of great leaders. Let us analyze fear and how this can be overcome.

Fear is a limited state of understanding – it is a state where you believe that we do not have enough or we will not receive something. After reading about Faith in the previous chapter, it would now be easy to understand that Fear is a lack of faith – when you have doubts and worry. Doubt and worry are lower-order vibrations and will pull you down the Awareness frequency ladder. As explained earlier, the lower you go down in the frequency ladder, the lesser you vibrate, gravitating towards destruction, disease, and decay. For example, studies have shown that being in a fearful state for a prolonged period could cause cancer. Even if one thinks that cancer may have a genetic trigger, the fact that they have a genetic potential to develop cancer triggers fear in their subconscious, and even this is passed onto the next generation through genes. In her book titled *Dying to be Me*, the Hong Kong-based Author Anita Moorjani narrates her true life story of how she died of 4th stage cancer and returned to life after a Near Death Experience when her father in heaven told her to '*Go back and live fearlessly*'. She states, "I had the choice to come back… or not. I chose to return when I realized that heaven is a state, not a place…."

Fear holds us back from the life that we truly desire. A toddler, for example, is not afraid of fire unless someone puts the fear in his mind. Babies are natural risk takers; we are born as natural risk takers, you and me. As we grow up, we are tied down by the shackles of paradigms and fearful beliefs – beliefs about money, careers, health, lifestyle, people, and so on.

We slowly lose track of which beliefs are progressive and which are destructive until, one day, they become our habits. Habits determine action, and action determines results. When we understand how to use the fire, creating a controlled environment of switches and lighters, we are not afraid to use it as we know and trust the technology or the tools. Similarly, when we know how to control the flow of ferocious water or overflowing rivers by building dams, we can channelize the same power into irrigating farmlands and providing electricity. It is the study and understanding that alleviates fear. Taking no action is not progressive. Abraham Maslow very beautifully said – ***You are either going to step forward in growth or step back into safety.***

There is no compensation in playing it safe. What happens if you are in fear and don't take that step forward – what do you lose? Here is my take on it. Technology is progressing; time is moving forward, and people around us, society, and culture are also progressing. In this scenario, if we refuse to grow and expand but stay in the same safe place, it is equivalent to moving backward. We will soon be thrown out of life's balance due to the void created by not following the law of spiritual expansion, which could affect us in many ways. It could be low self-esteem, it could be financial dependence, it could be the inability to make decisions, and so on. These can cause anxiety and depression. Emotions being electrical impulses in the nervous system that must be expressed through one thing you live in - that is, in your body – and that's the cause of anxiety – not knowing or uncertainty. If you are courageous, your emotional power is channelized into action and great results; that is the right flow of energy. Emerson said, **"Do the thing you want to do, and you will get energy to do it."** This is the only way to alleviate fear.

All you need to do is to take that one step forward, and then the next steps become automatically clear. Courage is that emotional trigger that is picked up and interpreted by the universal intelligence that I am ready to receive. You take one step, and the universe helps you with the subsequent steps. That is how it works.

To explain Fear in a more scientific manner, I would like to reference again to the Psycho-Cybernetics discussed earlier in this book. Whenever we try to change something, we are stuck with the dilemma of decision-making and a bolt of fear. ***The fear of the Unknown.*** In such a scenario, the only thing that will allow us to make the change and manage the fear is Awareness and Understanding of the expected results. Below is a simple table that illustrates the concept of fear and how to overcome it:

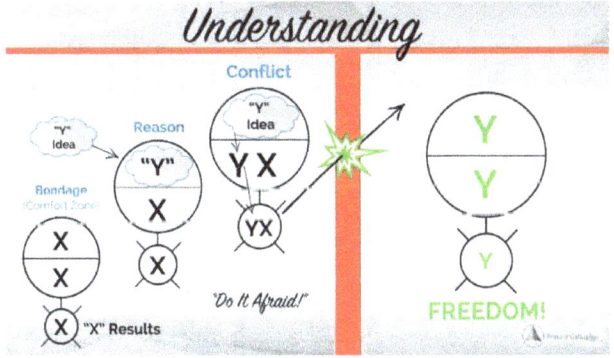

Source: PGI Coaching – Winner's Image Seminar

Let us analyze this illustration with an imaginary example. Alex has X-type thought – which is his current set of actions and comfort zone. He wants to change his results, as his current comfort zone will surely not give the desired results. He can choose to remain comfortable in getting inferior results – whether his income, a relationship, or whatever. Because he is afraid of change – this is his prison. The X-type thought produces X-type behavior and the same results. But when he tries to implement the Y idea, he is inflicted with the terror barrier – a mental conflict, fear, doubt, and anxiety, and he steps back into safety. His old beliefs and paradigms give him one hundred reasons not to take the next step. He thinks of hundred excuses not to take that one step.

However, with understanding and new awareness, he can break through the barrier to new freedom. As Henry David Thoreau has pointed out – ***"If one advances confidently in the direction of his dreams, and endeavors to live the life which he has imagined, he will meet with success unexpectedly in common hours."***

Bust through the terror barrier by being a little better every day – living new life every day, renewing and revving your thoughts every day. Every time you adopt and cross over to the other side of the terror barrier, you become a better, wiser, more confident, and more successful you. So, what will help us to break through the shackles of fear, worry, and doubt? Understanding. Hence my conclusion:

Courage comes from the place of Understanding, and Fear comes from the place of Lack of Awareness.

Understanding that it is truly fear that holds you back and not circumstances, using the reasoning and imagination faculty to chalk out a broad plan as to What we want, When we want, and How we will go about it – and then proceed fearlessly with faith. That is Courage. So, Courage really is not the absence of Fear, but Courage is a junction where Understanding and Faith meet, giving clear signage to success path. In other words, Courage is an antidote to Fear.

With this awareness, we can start setting higher and more ambitious goals and keep progressing. Normally, we do act and prepare everything, but when the time comes to really move forward or take that final step, we move back to safety as fear arises and we back off. This kind of safety is a self-designed prison. So, courage really is taking that one step forward – *Risk must be taken.* The greatest hazard in life is to risk nothing – as a person who risks nothing does nothing and gets nothing. You cannot live, love, and grow without taking risks; only a person who takes risks will enjoy the pleasure of true freedom.

The habit of thinking about oneself as a victim of circumstances and environment is as good as a prison – a self-designed prison. We can choose to think of our environment as a prison or a paradise. People become rich because they think and feel rich and abundant; some are free and open to change easily, while others feel safe in monotony; some seek opportunity while others wait for it to knock. Negative thinking shuts us in prison. The only way to transform is by the renewal of your mind repeatedly, by continually embracing newer, improved ideas, and crossing the terror barrier repeatedly. After achieving every goal, you must learn and grow again, ready to face the next terror barrier. That is the Progressive Realization of the goal – as defined in the first chapter – success mantra. This renewed person and rewiring of the mind, over and over again, is *Resurrection.* Every time you tread over fear and move forward, it is a new, bigger, and better YOU. That is true progress. This will automatically result in a change in your physical results, like money or assets, but that is the ***result*** of a physical measure of your growth. What you truly gain is growth in your Awareness level. In other words: **Your level of awareness defines your success!**

Most of us are conditioned to see the physical and material results that control our thinking – but we now know there are two options – An ignorant person lets the result control their thinking; they forget the goal and start to worry, which leads to fear. Eliminate ignorance by studying and developing awareness. Do not let the outside world and present results control your thinking. Understanding leads to faith, and that can transform your health and well-being. As Jacqueline Woodson stated: **In all your getting, get understanding.**

Alleviate fear by Faith and Courage - A higher-order vibration always destroys a lower-order vibration. This is the secret route to better ideas, better relationships, better results, more abundance, more success, and a fuller, more blissful life – more success! Let me repeat - One must know what he wants, when he wants, and more or less a rough idea as to how he must proceed to implement the plan. Once that is clear, one must proceed fearlessly in that direction.

As Friedrich Nietzsche beautifully put it - "**He who has a why to live can bear with almost any how.**" That is the only and sure path to success!

Chapter 9
Living Inside out - Imagination

If you fall in love with the imagination, you understand that it is a free spirit. It will go anywhere, and it can do anything!

Alice Walker

She was clearly talking about the Law of Attraction. Let us look at this more closely. The Law of Conservation of Energy states that Energy *cannot be created or destroyed – only converted from one form to another.* And from the theological sources, we know that: Exodus 16:22–30; Hebrews 4:1–11 – "Thus the heavens and the earth were completed in all their vast array. And by the seventh day, God had finished the work He had been doing, and so, on that day, He rested from all His Work."

God's work is completed. The creator created everything, small and big creatures, and also the pattern plan that provided the mechanisms to reproduce and keep alive his work of creation by changing forms, advancing, and evolving. It is not only true that the egg comes from the hen and vice versa, but all things change form. Ice turns to water upon melting, evaporates into steam upon heating, and finally vanishes into the ether but, upon condensation, will fall back onto earth as rain.

Thus, the formal substance remains intact but keeps changing its form. This is the law of Reversibility. This is, in fact, the same principle applied in all modern devices - A telephone converts the sound of a human voice into electronic signals that are transmitted via cables and other communication channels to another telephone which reproduces the sound to the receiving user. So, this is a change of form which is reversible. Initially, we established that friction causes electricity, and later, when we found electricity could be used to create friction, we started using electricity to create all modern mechanical devices and tools.

The same is the case for Thought energy – rather, the power of Imagination. It has been scientifically and beyond doubt proven that - Thought is a form of energy that transcends all time and space and is cosmic and potent. It can flash from pole to pole from one end of the world to the other in less than a second. Most important of all, thoughts can create things. If Things create thought, Thoughts can also create things. The Wright Brothers *imagined* and believed that they could devise a flying machine and created their first flying plane, which just flew for 15 seconds in December 1903. They first had it in their head and then in their hands.

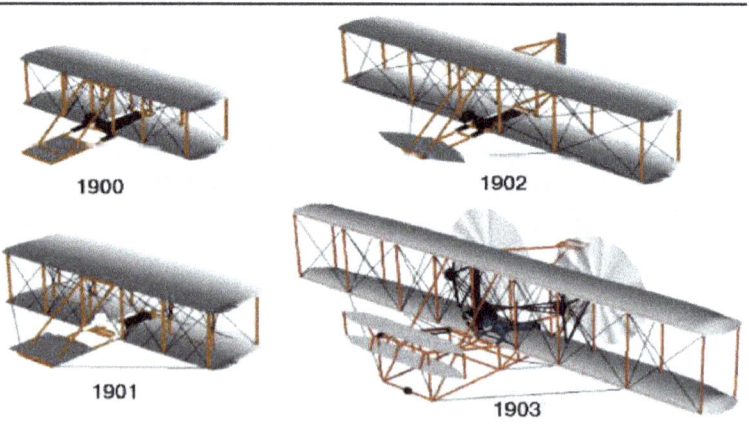

The Wright Brothers Aircraft – source Glenn Research Center - Wikipedia

All the things that we see around us, whether the table lamp, the table, your motor car, food, water bottle, cell phones and laptop, and even the building in which you are currently sitting, were originally a thought and then turned into reality by study, focus, belief, and pure and clear intention to create and deliver. So, Imagination is indeed the preview of life's coming attractions, as stated by Sir Albert Einstein. When we say imagination, we are referring to pure desire developed into things in the space of mind using the imagination faculty and then passionately and emotionally getting involved in the thought through study and focus, which will result in great production. The creation could be anything – a spick and span cleaning service, a best-in-class food delivery service, an invention, a newspaper journal, a new discovery, learning a new skill, and so on. But one must Imagine the desired result first. Then believe and get emotionally involved. This is the only way for beautiful and eternal creations.

Why must we create? Why is creation important for a successful and blissful life? Why do we have to live inside out? Why cannot we just live as per the happenings every day? The simple answer is – you are not following the law. Our only task and core purpose, being born as humans, is to work on progress and bettering what we are and what we have day by day. The fundamental purpose of the ever-expanding universe is to ensure all its creations also change, expand and grow. God's secret is encompassed even within the tiny pollen dust, which is not even visible to the naked eye. Yet it contains the divine formula and knows the pattern plan to stick to the stigma from the anther using a bee or wind as an interdependent agent, travels down the style of the flower to the ovary, fertilizes the ovules to produce the seed and the fruit from which the next new baby plant will sprout. So, everything, including humans, has been designed to create, recreate, and produce - it's the Law. However, due to the heightened faculties that we humans possess, that is, the ability to raise our awareness, it is expected we live life in a thriving mode and not as an animal in survival mode. In other words – Our level of Awareness defines our success and progress. Of course, it will take a very long time to reach the level of awareness and thought from which the earth was created, but at least we can try.

Living Inside Out also means living your true self, living as per your true call and purpose for which you are here on this earth, living freely, and aligning yourself to your soul's sincere desire. Not being in a creative state can cause an unexplained mental void which will lead to stress, discontent, anxiety, irritability, attitude, behavior, and, more importantly, health issues. Let us say a child loves to read books, and if we remove all the books from his home, it will create dissatisfaction and void, unfulfillment, and possibly character transformation too. How many things in a day which you do is really driven by an internal requirement for you or based on a requirement from someone else or for someone else or to please someone else? I mean, things that are taking away your time from focusing and working on your personal growth? Things that are unproductive and not aligned with your purpose. If that is the case, it is not the right approach and is not aligned with the laws of the universe. You must feed your soul first.

This by no means implies we should not help one another or support each other. But if you are aligned with your true inner self, it will magically become effortless and easy to be able to live and let live, get help and give support to as many people as you want simply because you are truly in a state of positive vibration. Every thought you entertain changes your vibration; hence, the only responsibility we have is to follow and persist on the right thought – when we are in that creative, producing, and giving frequency, the spirit will reciprocate in like kind. It may not be known how, when and from whom it will come back – the universal intelligence will decide. Your responsibility is to simply put out that idea, persist in the thought, and work towards your goal. What is the state of your vibration now? What are your thoughts, feelings, and action towards your business, personal, and family? Which thoughts would you like to keep, and which ones will be discarded? Living inside out is not letting your circumstances affect your ability to perform or waiver from your goal. In this context, I would love to give three of the world's best-known examples of those who have truly lived inside out and made a dramatic difference in the world.

Given below is an excerpt from the book Man's search for meaning by Dr. Viktor Frankl, whose story was narrated earlier in Chapter 4 – this is very interesting and self-explanatory:

"We who lived in concentration camps can remember the men who walked through the huts comforting others, giving away their last piece of bread. They may have been few, but they offer sufficient proof that everything can be taken from a man but one thing: the last of the human freedoms - to choose one's attitude in any given set of circumstances, to choose one's own way. Even though conditions such as lack of sleep, insufficient food and various mental stresses may suggest that the inmates were bound to react in certain ways, in the final analysis it becomes clear that the sort of person the prisoner became was the result of an inner decision, and not the result of camp influences alone. Fundamentally, therefore, any man can, even under such circumstances, decide what shall become of him - mentally and spiritually. He may retain his human dignity even in a concentration camp. Dostoevski said once, "There is only one thing that I dread: not to be worthy of my

sufferings." These words frequently came to my mind after I became acquainted with those martyrs whose behavior in camp, whose suffering and death, bore witness to the fact that the last inner freedom cannot be lost."

Dr. Frankl believed that man is even ready to suffer, on the condition, of being sure that his suffering has meaning. It is not compulsory, though, that he must suffer to find meaning and purpose. As we can see from this example, we humans are not fully conditioned and determined but can determine ourselves whether we give in to conditions or stands up to them. In other words, man is self-determining. Man does not simply exist but always decides what his existence will be, what he will become in the next moment, by his thoughts. However, most of us are not aware of this until we read this kind of book or hear from wise men. Simply put, *happiness cannot be pursued; it must ensue*. One must have a reason to "be happy." Once the reason is found, one becomes happy automatically. It means becoming aware of many possibilities against the background of reality or becoming aware of what can be done about a given situation.

The next example I would like to give is that of the Father of the Indian nation – Mahatma Gandhi – a non-violent activist and freedom fighter who liberated India from British Rule despite several years of imprisonment. He was by far the strongest symbol of non-violence in the 20th century. Mahatma Gandhi's most famous quote is '***Be the change you want to see.***' which is the clear translation of '**Living inside out.**'

Interestingly, Nelson Mandela, the South African Civil Rights Leader who was imprisoned for 27 years, also meant the same thing when he said, "***A winner is a dreamer who never gives up.***" – it meant infinite possibilities. Mandela spent the first 18 of his 27 years in jail at the brutal Robben

Island prison. He was confined to a small cell without a bed and forced to do hard labor in a quarry. From there, he kept writing and managed to smuggle his 500-page biography out through a departing prisoner in 1976 post which he lost his study rights for four years. Through it all, Mandela's resolve remained unbroken, and he led a movement of civil disobedience at the prison that coerced South African officials into drastically improving conditions on Robben Island. He received Nobel Peace Prize subsequently. Sharing below a very motivating and enlightening piece of wisdom from Sir Thomas Troward:

"My mind is a center of Divine operation. The Divine operation is always for expansion and fuller expression, and this means the production of something beyond what has gone before, something entirely new, not included in past experience, though proceeding out of it by an orderly sequence of growth. Therefore, since the Divine cannot change its inherent nature, it must operate in the same manner in me; consequently, in my special world, of which I am the center, it will move forward to produce new conditions, always in advance of any that have gone before."

In the context of Living Inside Out, I would like to give my interpretation of this incredibly famous and beautiful painting *The Creation of Adam* rendered by Michelangelo in the 15th century. This most famous painting is understood to depict the fleeting touch of God's fingers creating Man, made in His own image. Careful observation of works of various talented artists, poets, scientists, wise men, philosophers, and even mythological stories directed toward one common truth – *that God and Man are one.* God created man to recreate his creation. Man has all the powers of creation as God, but God has very cleverly separated the conscious from the subconscious, the áatman from the Paratmaatman (in the Hindu philosophy), and the physical state from the ethereal state. The secret to being able to reach the ethereal or spiritual state is also inside of us. In practice, very few people intend to manifest spiritual or supreme intelligence, while the majority of humanity desires money, career, relationships, and so on. Therefore, manifestations happen at that level only. The more we seek, the more we will find. Applying the law of vibration and understanding the self-frequency is the cornerstone for living life inside out. America's richest man Andrew Carnegie told in 1900 as follows: *"Any idea that is held in the mind, that is emphasized, that is either feared or revered, will begin at once to cloth itself in the most convenient and appropriate form available."*

The below painting depicts both the creation of Adam by the Lord God and the reverse as well - handing over of the desire from Man to God, that is, from conscious to subconscious mind. The picture depicts several forms/beings underneath God. Those are the symbols of prior manifestations. God created man (Adam in this picture) with the intention to create his own life by emotionally connecting to universal intelligence and supreme divine awareness. They meet at the fingertips, where the exchange

between the conscious to the subconscious is depicted. Every conscious thought that is emotionally fed into the subconscious mind is taken up by the Father (universal intelligence) and converted into a reality – a manifestation. This is my understanding and explanation of Michelangelo's painting – an analogy – as it states in the Bible – *John 10: 30 My Father who has given them to Me is greater than all. No one can snatch them out of My Father's hand.* ***The Father and I are one***, which means the desire, once formed, and persisted with belief, will truly manifest, no matter what.

Chapter 10
Focus and Will

No problem can stand the assault of sustained thinking ...

- Voltaire

Will is simply a plan or intent to do something, while Focus is the ability to persistently dwell on a certain act or thought. Will is driven by beliefs and paradigms, while Focus is a skill that can be developed by practice. Will is a mental faculty inbuilt in all humans. Both Will and Focus are critical elements that significantly contribute towards one's success and hence included as a dedicated chapter in this book.

People want to do and have many things; they wish for it, they want it, they think they can have it, and they are willing to get it, yet something does not work out. They do not always get what they want. Someone has been looking for a suitable job for six months with no luck! Another one is hanging on to a relationship hoping it will get better, but nothing changes! A student who fails in a subject is willing to study hard and pass the subject next time but fails again; what is not working?

Here is the thing. Wanting something is one thing and being willing to accept it wholeheartedly is another. When you want to achieve something – then you must be *truly willing*; this means accepting that the result is yours and all other situations and circumstances with it should be fully acceptable to you. Are you willing to take the full responsibility that comes with your desires? If not, there will be a misalignment between wish and true intent, and it will delay the results. While the student is willing to improve, the question will be whether he is willing to accept the subject and open himself to learn it, gain more knowledge, and increase his awareness wholeheartedly. A struggling artist wants to grow his art business - he is willing to set up his studio and start his new business in the next big town, but is he ready to make a move wholeheartedly? Is he ready to receive a larger group of customers, face difficulties, and give his time, energy, and money to developing the business? If not, the desire will remain a dream.

Will, therefore actually means a true intent, and unless there isn't a Will, it is difficult to achieve any goal. The best example I could give is that from my own life. While I was still pulling up my finances to meet the criteria required to apply for the golden visa (long-term permanent residency) in UAE, I unexpectedly received the visa under a special category due to my accomplishments in this area. This was something I thought I would get ten years later, after my retirement from employment, but because of my true intention, the permit manifested several years ahead of my plan. You will never know how the universe works, but you will surely get what you strongly desire and genuinely intend. I wanted to be a writer – that remained a wish until I started writing. Whoever or whatever you want to become, you must be willing to accept fully that it is yours by demand, then manifestation becomes effortless and faster. There are many such examples in my life and have seen happening around me. The manifestations do not always go as per the exact plan; you may not get what you must get from the person whom it is expected. It can come from anywhere, anytime, in any form. If we have this awareness and do not worry or fret about the outcome, no one can stop us from becoming extraordinarily successful in everything we touch.

Abundance is a *blanket feeling*, and it does not just cover sufficient money but also covers fulfilling relations, a successful career, a progressive peer circle, and so on. Similarly, true intention is like a blanket feeling, and all things, people, plots, and plans needed to manifest what you intend get covered by it. Abundance is not always about money; hence return for your intention can come in different forms than you expect. Sometimes it is hard to comprehend certain things that occur in life; someone loses a job, someone loses a relationship, but when one looks back, they may realize that they may not have been where they are today without those events. This is exactly what Apple founder and CEO Steve Jobs mentioned in one of his famous speeches at Stanford University in 2005 *"You cannot connect the dots looking forward, you can only connect them looking backwards. So you have to trust that the dots will somehow connect in the future, you have to trust in something, yours guts, destiny, karma whatever…because believing the dots would connect down the road will give you the confidence to follow your heart, even if it leads you off the well-worn path, and that will make all the difference."*

Will, being a mental faculty, can be exercised and enhanced to our advantage. We can consciously put in *clear intention* into the things we speak, write, and do to get the desired positive result faster. For example, a salesman is emailing a sales quote to a customer. Obviously, he wants the customer to agree to his proposal. He needs to create the email with a positive mind frame and true intent, providing the best possible service for the quoted price. There should be no fear and worry but a feeling of gratitude for 1) being able to serve others and 2) for being able to accept this new relationship as a client.

This intention and feeling will move the communication to the level of frequency required to attract customer agreement. In other words - 'When there is a will, there is a way'. When true intent is put into something, the Universe opens the way automatically toward the manifestation of the desired state.

As seen in all the examples, with every will, there is entailing action required. We live in a physical world. A will needs to be supported by not only emotional energy but also physical energy of action. While the will speeds up manifestation, you still need to make that choice, take that decision, and step forward to reach the desired result. This is where *focus* comes in. Focus or concentration is the ability to direct one's attention toward following their goal. Will without focus is like soup without salt in it. To focus on something is to highlight something, is to persistently pay attention to it to achieve a specific goal or conclusion. Continued focus and persistent attention are imperative to drive a certain will to magnify its impact. Focus is a skill one can develop through continuous practice.

It is a simple science of mind. You always get those things done to which you pay attention. If your attention diverts into multiple unproductive, unrelated things during sitting at your work desk, you will find nothing can be accomplished by the end of the day. Everyone has experienced this. Your attention follows your thought, and your thought follows habits. If you really want to change the results in your life, you need to have focused and undivided attention on that thing to achieve the desired result. However, the focus is by far the biggest challenge most people face. Throughout the day, during travel to work, on bus or train, during a meeting, after getting up in the morning, before going to bed, and sometimes even in the washroom, we browse our phones to see if there are any new messages, downloads, news even if we are not expecting anything. This is because we have practiced doing this all the time; it is aimless, meaningless, and adds no value to the set goal.

Such habits make you look for excuses and deviate from the new plan or proposed lifestyle. Hence you give up and start procrastinating. This will obviously not lead to the desired result. You will have to develop new brain cells to change the habit - you will have to develop the skill of focusing. To change your habit, you must repeat a certain activity for a prolonged period, a few days to weeks. This will bring alignment between actions and goals, facilitating the transformation of a desire into a physical reality, like exercising a muscle to make it stronger - there can be no other way. There is a curriculum built in schools, colleges, and workplaces to help develop attention and focus skills. On certain days, you feel you were able to accomplish more, and others were unproductive and wasted. This is because you are too distracted to complete the set task for the day. Let us look at factors that may help to develop concentration and focus.

- Avoid distractions like phone calls or browsing the phone unless required for the task at hand

- Ensure sufficient sleep or rest at night and during the day to keep the brain cells well-charged. Like mobile phones, our brain and body also get recharged and reorganized when we are sleeping.

- Avoid multitasking – it does not mean that you cannot manage multiple projects at one time or multiple roles and responsibilities. It means at one point in time, you must focus completely on one action you are performing, whether a phone call, email, driving, or shopping, and when it is done, move on to the next task of the day. This way, not only does the job gets done quickly, but it will also have fewer mistakes and be stress-free as well. Allocating time or calendarizing your priorities relieves you of the stress of finishing everything at a time.

- To have more productive days – one of the simplest and key things to do is to prioritize as little as just ten things to do in a day instead of an extensive list. Focus on one at a time and complete them all by the end of the day. Taking it one day at a time is a sure and steady way to work towards success in any field. If you are busy with other commitments and cannot give an hour or two to the task, you may still do a five-minute part to set the intent out; you have still moved forward in the direction of your goal rather than not doing anything at all.

- There are games and brain exercises that also help in developing concentration and focus, such as jigsaw puzzles, sudoku, chess, and video games.

To sum it up, one must understand the power of Will and set the intention wholeheartedly, then consciously focus on the action required to attain the desired goal. One must enjoy the process of performing the work more than the desired result – this will improve the quality of the desired result. The term *Nishkam Karma* from the Bhagavat Gita is quite commonly misunderstood to mean working without any desire – but I would rather interpret it differently – it means focusing on the present moment wholeheartedly with the *true intention* of providing genuine service or goods, not worrying about the result – by the complete surrender into the action itself to make best possible creation. No man wants to be greedy or selfish and keep everything to himself, denying others their rights to share. We get a great true sense of accomplishment when we can create, serve, provide, give, show, and prove something that truly benefits everyone around us.

Everyone knows they cannot carry their physical wealth and gains with them when they die – however, two things can make a man greedy for money or food, i.e., (1) insecurity and (2) habit. Insecurity arises from a lack of awareness, and habits can change by working on self-image. If we realize that we are all connected and sourced from one universal energy, then no one must feel insecure or inferior, as there is infinite abundance everywhere around us – we can see it only if we believe in it and are willing to receive it. To be able to remain focused and keep on delivering without worry, we need to have the assurance that all that transpires will be good, or at least we should condition the mind to believe that it is the case. We can do this easily by practicing the powerful technique of Generative Gratitude discussed in the next chapter.

Always Remember, your focus determines your reality – George Lucas.

Chapter 11
Generative Gratitude

We have repeatedly been bombarded with advice from all corners; since early childhood about the importance of practicing gratitude – elders in the family, coach, friends, relatives, and even in corporate life, we have Gratitude Thursdays. People tend to follow these as rituals and say *Thank you* to one another as a matter of practice. But very few understand the purpose and science behind being grateful.

There is a Law of Gratitude, just like other laws of life. This chapter intends to elucidate how this law works and why being in a state of gratitude is important to achieve continuous success. In the earlier chapter, we discussed the emotional pyramid. We also read and understood that it is important to be in a higher frequency to attract all good things in life and how by managing your emotions, you can continue to keep yourself in good vibes prolonging your stay in higher frequency as much as possible.

Throughout the day, we keep moving up and down the frequency ladder by virtue of our thoughts and related emotions. Sometimes we are joyous, sometimes angry, sometimes anxious or worried, and sometimes relaxed. Every thought and resulting emotion that has been the most impactful during the day is picked up by the subconscious mind, and at night during sleep, when the conscious mind has done all the handing over of its work to the subconscious, the latter connects to the universal intelligence and creates the pattern plan of manifesting whatever has been the key ask through the prominent feelings during the day. That's why they say: *You don't get what you want, but you get what you are.* That is, whatever you are by your feelings.

In this context, I would like to narrate a story depicted in the autobiography of former President of India, the Late Dr. A P J Abdul Kalam, in the book *Wings of Fire*. In his youthful days, Dr. Abdul Kalam had an ardent desire to join the Indian Air Force. The author beautifully depicts how he proceeded with the interview in Dehradun, where the emphasis was more on personality than intelligence; perhaps they were looking for more physical fitness and an articulate manner. He clearly explains his mixed emotions – excited but nervous, determined but anxious, confident but tense and goes on to state that he could only finish 9th in the hatch of 25 officers examined to select eight officers for commissioning in the Airforce. Indeed, he was extremely disappointed and proceeded on his way to Rishikesh, the mighty Himalayan mountains which have been visited through centuries by sadhus and pilgrims to seek peace and wisdom. He landed at the Sivananda Ashram, where Swami Sivananda, who could without even speaking to young Abdul Kalam, gauge his grief and here's what he said when he heard his story about not being selected for the Airforce:

"Desire, when it stems from the heart and spirit, when it is pure and intense, possesses awesome electromagnetic energy. This energy is released into the ether each night, as the mind falls into the sleep state. Each morning it returns to the conscious state reinforced with cosmic currents. That which has been imaged will surely and certainly be manifested. You can rely, young man, upon ageless promise as surely as you can rely upon the eternally unbroken promise of sunrise…and Spring."

What a profound revelation! From the perspective of manifestation, we can argue that he was physically not aligned to the position in the Airforce. But he had a powerful desire to soar high and serve the country – it was merely his perception at the point in time that the most coveted and prestigious way to serve the country would be to join the Air Force. He got the profound revelation from the Swami to *accept his destiny and go ahead with his life – that he is not destined to become an Airforce pilot – what he is destined to become is not revealed now but already pre-determined – forget the failure as it was essential to lead him to his destined path.* Dr. APJ Abdul Kalam later went on to become an Aerospace Scientist and Statesman serving as the 11th President of India between 2002 and 2007. Many years later, when he became a statesman, he was finally able to do a six-month course and fly the coveted aircraft too!

Sometimes, it does not matter whether a certain goal is achieved, but the sure and tested tool to be in a good vibration is to let go, to free the mind from fear, worry, and anxiety, replacing these emotions with more positive and higher order emotions. It is indeed difficult to smile amidst adversities, to be happy when you lose something and when time turns against you. How can one do that?

Gratitude is an easy-to-use tool for this purpose. By practicing gratitude, you are reminding yourself to be happy, joyous, and grateful for the beautiful and precious things you already have in life. It is a technique to take attention away from feeling disappointed and fearful and put you onto a higher frequency by placing a belief in something or someone, whereby you know that what you desire is already and truly yours. It is a simple tool and amazingly easy to practice anytime, anywhere, as many times as you want, and it is free. We teach children to say 'Thank You' which subconsciously develops the habit of gratefulness, but as we grow up, it becomes just a mechanical ritual with no binding emotions, at least not every time we say the words.

Gratitude is a tried and tested tool to be in a good vibration. But what is the right way to practice it, and how can we ensure it will work for us? Here, let me introduce the concept of Generative Gratitude. I learned the concept of Generative gratitude from my mentor Mary Morrissey. There are two types of gratitude – (1) Knee jerk Gratitude and (2) Generative gratitude. When you thank someone for something they have done or given, like service or sales, it is in return for something you have already received, and it's a reaction to an event that precedes you feeling grateful. This is knee-jerk or reactive gratitude. This is more of a social formality and surely makes both parties feel good, but this is not a major contributor if you must invoke the law of attraction. So, we need to understand Generative Gratitude.

Generative Gratitude means you can generate or create an infinite amount of gratitude from within you. It means acknowledging everything that you are, you have, you do, and you get your entire life, including the people around you. Grateful for being a part of God's creation and for being able to create, produce, and give. If you start looking at your life in this manner, you will never really be able to stop writing down the list of things you are blessed with, right from acknowledging every little piece of bone, organs, and cells in your body to the air you breathe, your house, motor, mobile, relationships, books you read, your ability to think, mental faculties, and the list goes on and on.

Generative gratitude really points to our ability to create a feeling of awe, joy, and gratefulness within ourselves for everything that we have and even for things that have still not manifested in life. It, therefore, binds in hope and faith too. This explains why sometimes we receive an unexpected benefit or gain, which leaves us wondering with delight – *When did I even pray or ask for this – it is simply amazing!* It could be a kind word from a friend, an unexpected bonus, a new car at an unbelievable price, anything. All these circumstances happen serendipitously. It automatically makes you feel happy and grateful for receiving such unexpected gain, and because you are happy and grateful for that, you will attract more joy and manifestations. It produces a snowball effect. This explains the following verse:

Give, and it will be given to you. They will pour into your lap a good measure–pressed down, shaken together, and running over

(Luke 6:38, NASB)

Give, stated above, in my interpretation, does not refer to giving money to a religious or charitable body or helping someone who has no value for it financially because that will not really lift anyone from a state of poverty or misery. Give actually refer to **Giving love**, even if it is our enemies, being non-judgmental, seeing them all alike; **Giving blessing** that is wishing good for others the way you wish for yourself, treating others the way you wish to be treated, and; **Giving release**, that is forgive and let go if someone has wronged you and sometimes even forgive yourself. These are indeed difficult things to practice, but by doing these, you are not only ensuring that you are keeping yourself in the open, receiving mode but are truly helping and lifting others up along with you.

The simplest, most straightforward way to ensure applying all three above types of *Giving* is to be in a state of *generative gratitude*. When you practice generative gratitude, you are automatically non-judgmental about people and circumstances, your faith is heightened, and you release yourself from guilt, shame, and anger by forgiving too. Do you see how powerful this tool is, then? The three most lethal emotions, *guilt, fear, and anger,* can be reduced greatly by one simple practice or tool. Isn't that truly thrilling? This also binds back to the Law of Receiving explained earlier.

The theological statement mentioned above, **Luke 6.38,** also has an amazing likelihood of the simple process of child conception. We manifest a child through the same sequence stated above – it happens when the male life source – sperm, is *given* unto the female life source – the ovum. Intent precedes a conception before it results in a manifestation. Such a simple secret of gratitude embodied in our life, but we totally miss seeing it – a simple secret intertwined in our lives!!

Just by raising your awareness, you will understand that your source of joy, happiness, and satisfaction does not come from outside of you but is sourced from what you have been thinking and feeling. The good news is, however, you can change your feelings by changing your thoughts – instantly, like snapping of the fingers!!! That is by manipulating your emotions. Gratitude is a tool for that manipulation. So, along with being grateful for all the good and beautiful things in life, wholistically acknowledge everything in life – whether you perceive it good or not, acknowledge and be thankful for it because it is all part of a pattern plan for you to get what you desire, for you to succeed in manifesting your desires. Life then will appear full of miracles and blessings for you and everyone else around you whom you meet.

It is a good practice to keep a gratitude journal where you can spend 3-5 minutes every day listing down your gratitude statements, or you could also be part of peer groups that share gratitude statements with each other every day – it is good to make this a daily practice, so this soon becomes a subconscious habit automatically converting us into a more optimistic person. A few powerful gratitude statements are listed below as examples; these are taken from various sources from mentors and motivators:

- *I am so happy and grateful that I am the creator of my life. Every choice, action, and feeling contributes to my beautiful life.*

- *I am so happy and grateful that I made the decision to change my mindset so that I can attract all the good into my life constantly by rising to its frequency.*

- *I am so happy and grateful that I am raising my awareness every day and sharing my positive vibes with as many people around me as possible*

- *I am so happy and grateful now that money comes to me in increasing quantities through multiple legitimate sources on a continuous basis.*

- *I am so happy and grateful that my Life is full of pleasant surprises " I love who I am, I love what I do and I love who I am becoming."*

You can also add things that have not yet manifested in your life to this list, and this will help to achieve success even faster.

Chapter 12
Calmness of Mind

What does Calmness of Mind mean? What role does it play in our success journey and our life as a whole? The calmness of mind is a state of being able to stay serene, cutting down the noise of distractions. Thoughts flow into our mind all the time, some create deep emotions, and some pass away just like that, but the calmness of the mind is vitally important to be able to make use of the creative energy within us and bring out our full inner potential.

When an artist creates a masterpiece, when you are drafting a deal-breaking email, or when athletes win races, calmness of mind is particularly important. It is important to be able to get great results and produce high-quality work or service. I would like to state here a sentence from the last chapter of Serenity in the *Book As a Man Thinketh* by James Allen, also stated in the last chapter of my previous book Thinking into Desires:

"Calmness of Mind is one of the beautiful jewels of wisdom. It is the result of long and patient effort in self-control. Its presence is an indication of ripened experience, and of a more than ordinary knowledge of the laws and operations of thought."

It is indicative of how one has transitioned from an animal-like awareness to a state of Mastery. It demonstrates utmost self-control and the ability to stay focused on one purpose, one worthy ideal, and one goal at a time. The calmness of mind is needed to be able to think deeply and make full use of the mental faculties. Here is a scientific explanation for those who struggle to understand the correlation between a calm mind and success. Let us review the Science of Brainwaves a little bit here. The EEG (electroencephalograph) measures brainwaves of different frequencies within the brain. Based on studies and research conducted, there are four broad frequency bands, i.e., Gamma greater than 30(Hz), BETA (13-30Hz), ALPHA (8-12 Hz), THETA (4-8 Hz), and DELTA (less than 4 Hz).

The **Delta** state is the sleep or drowsy state when there are no conscious activities. The **Theta** state is when we transition to a sleep-like state from the awakened state – it has slow mental activity and is seen in connection with creativity, intuition, daydreaming, and fantasizing and is a repository for memories, emotions, and sensations. In this state, we can access universal intelligence to draw wisdom from it and create a belief or image in the subconscious. We become one with our true selves during the Theta state. This is what Van Gogh would have experienced when he stated: *I dream my paintings, and then I paint my dreams.*

In the **Alpha** state, one can use his/her full potential, efficient accomplishments, and mental coordination, and it is a bridge-like state between the conscious and the subconscious mind. It is a common state when the person is alert and is one of the brain's most important frequencies to learn and use the information learned. Alpha-Theta training can create an increase in sensation, abstract thinking, and self-control. Beta and Gamma are for more efficient and higher performance of the brain.

A calm mind increases the ability to focus, both inwards and outwards, on self and others. This state also helps to connect to the subconscious when ideas and wisdom flow into consciousness effortlessly. By manipulating the states of mind, we can achieve the desired change in personality or talent needed to perform certain tasks. Steve Woods is a Golf Hypnotist who helps unprofessional players to become better by removing mental blocks. He trains not on the technical part of Golf but just on the mindset part of it. He explains that sometimes players overthink or suffer from First Tee Nerves, the Yips, or Shanks. He offers hypnosis as a rapid and effective way to change the performance mindset. Similar treatment is also given to children suffering from attention syndrome and other abnormal frequencies of the brain waves. The calmness of the mind can be developed by practice over a period.

Everybody likes the company of calm people around them. As one's wisdom grows and awareness expands, one automatically becomes calmer and more confident. They are looked upon as leaders, perceived to have demonstrated great self-control and resilience in the face of adversities. People flock around them for advice and mentorship. They become walking magnets attracting more success in their endeavors and inspiring others. Lack of calmness of mind directly results in low focus, low productivity, low self-esteem, and poor results.

But as stated earlier, there are techniques and tools that we can apply to calm a chaotic state, whether it is related to finance, relationship, career, or anything. If bankers, healthcare professionals, athletes, and other high-stress-prone workers perform the same tasks that they do every day with an altered state of mind, that is, by cultivating a restful, relaxed, it will bring them greater attention, creativity, and energy to tackle the varied challenges.

One of the best examples I can give is by sharing my own experience. Considering that I juggle various roles such as banking risk manager, researcher, writer, speaker, artist, entrepreneur, personal development coach, and mother (and a wife, too), I often get the feeling of being unproductive when certain tasks are not done within a targeted timeframe.

I end up feeling guilty, less powerful, and de-motivated. But after I studied and became aware of the application of calmness of mind, my productivity and speed of accomplishment saw dramatic improvements. I realized that being calm helps to channel all energy and intent into one task, which results in both high-quality product or service and completion well in advance of time – in other words, accomplishment becomes effortless and hence less stressful. I have applied, tried, and assessed this in many matters in life, big or small, and would urge all readers to pay particular attention to this chapter.

A stressed mind is unable to produce undivided attention because there is the demon of pressure hovering over you from behind – the pressure could be in any form, a target date, a report without errors, an approval on some critical decision, fear of losing something, worry about the effect on the audience, and so on. Because stress narrows down the focus, we tend to close part of the mind and reduce our ability to perform with an open mindset in whatever we endeavor. Calming the mind down in such situations helps us to dissolve the feeling of pressure and hence provides more energy to perform better and to the fullest, opening our minds and perception to unlimited possibilities, which in turn makes accomplishing tasks efficient, excellent, and effortless. The availability of wholesome energy helps us to be more present, which alters our state of mind. Let us look at techniques and tips that can be applied to develop and retain calmness of mind.

Breathing: The simplest and age-old technique is using our breath. We can change how we feel by changing the way we breathe. Because breathing (air) is one of the vital life sources of energy, learning to regulate breathing will help us to regulate the way we perceive things and hence the results in our life. In Chinese, it is called Chi; in Japanese, Ki; and in Sanskrit, Prana. There are various courses and mentorship available across the globe to learn and master this practice. But this book aims to make it simpler for the readers by sharing tips that are both accessible and free. One of the most calming breathing exercises you can do is to breathe in (e.g., to a count of four), hold, and then breathe out for up to twice as long (e.g., to a count of six or eight). The long exhale of the parasympathetic nervous system reduces the heart rate and blood pressure.

Compassion: Exercising compassion towards self and others will immediately relieve us from worry, stress, and frustration. Compassion means being accepting, kind, and non-critical about something or someone. Mostly, we are stressed by the invisible chains of our beliefs and perceptions. For example, if I must deliver an excellent quality management presentation within a certain date, the worry that it may not fully meet the audience's needs and that I may not be able to finish on time will induce stress and lower the quality of input in work. But if I can exercise compassion for myself, if I can be less judgmental or critical and be appreciative of my efforts, this will melt the invisible chains of stress, calm me down, and my performance will be more effortless, faster, and of better quality due to availability of full energy to do the task. Similarly, if you are expecting satisfactory results from a peer, your subordinate, your spouse, or your child and you put worry or fear into it, it sends a signal of mistrust and low confidence, in turn affecting their performance too. Therefore, being compassionate and kind is critical to calm down the mind quickly and easily.

Self-talk or Inner conversations are by far the most powerful, and one of my favorite techniques used not just to calm the mind but also for other personality and self-image development programs or projects. When in a difficult or anxious situation, simply a strong, emotional, powerful self-talk statement, such as "Calm down, all is well…" immediately changes the frequency of your being into a positive mental state. There are affirmation statements that can be made, such as:

"You will crack it on time."

"You are always a winner."

"All is well; keep going."

"Well done! Now let's move on to the next."

"You are amazing! Achiever."

Affirmations should be made with deep feelings and emotions toward the self. Every strong emotional release is like a wave of energy. Anything stated or wished with strong emotion will manifest in the quickest and most convenient conceivable way. So, when we are down with a negative emotion, the best way to deal with it is by making a counter statement with a positive emotion. This really works. And very well too! I would like to end the chapter with the wisdom quote as follows:

"You never change something by fighting the existing reality. To change something, build a new model that makes the old model obsolete." – R. Buckminster Fuller.

Are you ready to transform the results in your life? All you need is a worthy ideal, intent to give your all, and an appetite to grow bigger, better, stronger, and to become a new, more successful you!!! Start thinking differently from today.

About the Author

Suryaprabha Easwar is a Dubai-based entrepreneur and researcher on the Laws of Life, dedicated to sharing her life-transformative insights worldwide through mentoring programs, public speeches, and writing. Her motto is to raise public awareness by propagating the concept of living *Inside Out,* exploring the fullest inner potential, which is the secret of true bliss and success, making life more meaningful and worthy for the seekers!

suryaprabhae@gmail.com.

www.ingramcontent.com/pod-product-compliance
Lightning Source LLC
Chambersburg PA
CBHW072102110526
44590CB00018B/3284